Cariappa Annaiah is a self-taught, eclectic poet and artist, and mentor based in Greater New Orleans. A physician by training and an anatomic pathologist by specialization, he worked as a scientist in India for eight years and in Massachusetts for 22 years before relocating south ten years ago.

He holds the earned designation of Copley artist at the Copley Society of Art in Boston, the oldest nonprofit art association in America. He is a member of The New England Poetry Club, founded by Amy Lowell, Robert Frost, and Conrad Aiken in 1915. A published poet and award-winning artist, his artwork is in private collections in the USA and abroad.

View his unique artwork at www.cariappa.net.

(Photo credit: Self-portrait; Copyright © 2023 Cariappa Annaiah)

Also by Cariappa Annaiah

Echoes of Epictetus & Arrian
Illustrations – Warsha Lath

Truisms – mostly
Reflections on life, living, and relationships

Truisms – mostly
Volume II
Reflections on life, living, and relationships

Irregularly Irregular

Further reflections on life, living, and relationships for a reflective audience

Cariappa Annaiah

InwardStep Publications

Copyright © 2024 Cariappa Annaiah. All rights reserved.

Cover design: Cariappa Annaiah
Cover illustration: Thoth And Ra, original fine art work, Cariappa Annaiah.

First edition
Printed in the United States of America

InwardStep Publications
Mandeville, LA
Web site: www.inwardsteppublications.com

ISBN: 978-0-9845462-3-7

Library of Congress Control Number: 2024918753

All rights reserved. This book, or parts thereof, may not be reproduced in any form without the written permission of the author except in the case of brief quotations in critical articles and reviews. These poems may not be set to music without permission. This is the only authorized first edition of this collection, so please do not purchase or distribute illegal copies or encourage piracy of the copyrighted materials in this book. For more information contact InwardStep Publications through the above website.

Contents

Dedication	ix
Introduction	xi
Formatting Note	xiii
Poems	1
Acknowledgments	289
Subject Index	291
Title Index	313

Dedication

Guddi who showed me how to live, recover from loss, and die gracefully.

Andrew who had the vision to give me a blue-sky opportunity that, in retrospect, I had trained, unbeknownst to me, for 30 years.

Cissy who continues to demonstrate by example how to keep active, grow your mind, and contribute throughout life (as long as health is okay).

From anywhere with love

R sweetheart,
You brought us together more than once and more than once is your preference!
Hail to the Queen of more than once!

Introduction

The focus of my poetry is relationships—personal, professional, and social. Why? Personal and professional happiness depends on the state of health of my relationship with myself, and then with others.

The poems are hyper-local. By counting from one and improving my ability to manage myself emotionally and physically, and then influencing others around me, I can make change one individual at a time, starting with myself. I keep my bar low! From my perspective, the only way to initiate long-term change is to work locally and walk the talk.

Why Irregularly Irregular?
Two reasons:
– Other than reflecting reality, my poetry and art cannot be typecast.
– Reality is unpredictable. Unlike fantasy, which is a captive of the mind and thusly malleable, ductile, and predictable since we are in charge, reality is our captor; we are at its mercy; it shapes us like putty and grudgingly yields to our hopes and aspirations.

And, why the warning *for a reflective audience*?
Again, reflecting reality, and different from my previous collections, these poems explore all nooks and crannies of the mind and body. From my perspective, refusing to identify and address elephants in the room and denying that sex is a physiological urge is the root of a lot of personal and social ills.

Unlike The Muses, my muses are more than 9! And many poems are footnoted, acknowledging the inspiration.

Ogden Nash, the American humorist, and Piet Hein, the Danish polymath, are my poetry heroes. Why? Their poetry is profundity wrapped in lightness.

Other influences are R. D. Laing, the Scottish psychiatrist, writer and poet, T. M. Raghuram, the Indian psychiatrist and poet, E. E. Cummings, the American freeformist, and Antonio Porchia, the Italian-born Argentinian poet.

From ecstasy to misery, success to failure, bathos to pathos, you will find a mirror on life in this collection.

Finally, a note about the cover art work, "Thoth And Ra" who are the ancient Egyptian moon and sun Gods. The border between light and gray, notice I did not say dark, is jagged and irregularly irregular!

Formatting Note

The poems, like reality, are aligned right, left or center. Capitalization, punctuation, and line discipline follow the rule—whatever makes the poem understandable. Poems running over a page continue on the facing page.

Irregularly Irregular

The Block In Thought

On the spectrum of thought
we get caught when we ought not to, by naught

circular thinking, mental blocks
magical thinking and whatnots.

Convenience Trap

For the harried, worried, scurried
conveniences are convenient

for the poor, overloaded, overdrawn
conveniences are life-changing

for the disabled
conveniences enable.

For the able who mostly have none of these labels
unlimited conveniences ultimately disable

they enable a slow, multigenerational slide
into dependency, complacency, and other negative tendencies

promising the Holy Grail of efficiency-driven multitasking
delivering sawdust aplenty and few cut logs

lots of action and few completions
nurtures impatience and dampens intentions.

Able with none of the labels
retain the essential ability to labor

muster conveniences that make your life better
while mastering manual and mental labor

limiting conveniences and practicing skills
nurtures patience, resilience, and critical skills.

The Ark Of Life

It is said, Noah said
come aboard two by two
creatures paired and boarded

commanding my own Life Boat
I commanded my qualities
come aboard two by two

wisdom, it is said, comes with age
sadly, for me, as Oscar said
age came alone.

Muse: JD and Oscar Wilde.

Discussion—The Lack Thereof

We
diss
cuss
shun

one another

no matter
what matter
all matters

Where to begin?

Our problems and us too tangled to untangle
disputed beginnings and no end in sight

a Gordian Knot* of weak, venal and vicious humans
no linchpin to help unravel and a sword handy.

---

*The Gordian Knot and Alexander the Great's solution. Reference: Wikipedia, "Gordian Knot," 2024, https://en.wikipedia.org/wiki/Gordian_Knot.

Hot And Frozen

My beloved is passionable
not actionable

Can I get a potion to spark some action
in my passionable nonactionable?

The Dilemma

In thrall to perfectionism

we build "perfect" teams

of competent adults

then, as perfectionists

we struggle—

yield control or control more.

Oh micromanager, as the saying goes

why keep a dog and bark yourself?

Oh, Humankind

when will we learn?
We blame wars and conflict on human-made weapons

Arms? We don't need them
We have two!

Arms preceded Arms
Who needs weapons, when we have two?

Weapons are a *force-multiplier*
We are a *conflict-multiplier*

if not race, then ethnicity
if not religion, then sect

if not resources, then jealousy
if not this, then that.

Face Value

Humans do it all the time
judge a book by the cover

headline turns me off
no patience for nuance

first impression
once and done

no interaction required
THOSE people look shady.

Folks get ready
to look as shady

not be read or listened to
by anybody

THOSE people
are just like you.

The Dice In Our Lives

sitting next to you
I hear you exhale as I inhale

your warmth and love
coming from the depths of your soul

Chance, luck, serendipity
call it whatever

here we are
taking deep breaths of one another.

This Is Love Too

When you say it's winter in summer
I say look at the pretty snow out there

When you are off to the circus still sitting in bed
I'm Jolly the Clown clowning for you

Stalking a lion in a big game hunt
I'm your tracker as you walk your dog

As mind slowly streams away from body
my love shapeshifts into a raft, and

floats in your stream too.

Giving Is Not A Given

On the spectrum of human behavior
self-centered focus is at one end
altruism on the other

Infants consume
adults give
don't assume movement

Some consume all their lives
others, consumed in the giving
both unaware that binary thinking is best in a bin

Retain self-worth, be a consumer and a giver
How will you know what you gave up
if you didn't consume what you give?

The Protected—A Public Service Reminder, For Parents, Politicians, And Policymakers

I will protect your mind
from the harms of reality

words you read
sanitized, your mind, sterile

sounds you hear
no dissonance, addicted to harmony

the sights you see
I will censor, mind sees no blood and gore

I will protect you, in complete denial
as you, naive novitiate, in adulthood

—runs headlong into Reality's knife, and bleeds
aghast at society-at-large, losing faith in Humanity

oppressed by anxiety
pressed down by depression—

as I blame all else, but self.

The Hurricane

Our relationship
like a hurricane, hurried and came

loosened our moorings
shredded logic

wiped out sanity
upended reality

blew out of our lives
as it blew up our lives

leaving behind for us to deal with
the love child of a nightmare and a circus.*

*Last line attributed to an anonymous source whose house was wrecked by a hurricane.

The Human Condition

Choices we make
choices we keep
at times, not the choices we want.

Nursing Hope

As my milk flows into you
may the milk of kindness, too

may you milk joy from all you do
and share that joy around you

be ready to make cheese and recover
when others unjustly spoil and curdle

But, right now, cuddley-duddle
just get on with it and fill your middle!

Dedicated to the bleary-eyed mothers and partners
awake at 3:00 a.m. feeding their dawdling bundle.

Traveler

Cross, we bear
is that cross we must
Crossroads of Life.

Enough Is Not Enough Or Is It?

I don't get to see you often enough
though we are close enough

I think of you often enough
but that is not enough

I know you well enough
to know that you reciprocate enough

My challenge is to make peace with what is enough
when I know that your life is equally busy enough

I promise to leave you well enough alone
so that you can determine how much is enough.

Accounting Error

Pointing fingers at others
so easy, low hanging fruit

We should improve
We? Multiple personalities, are we?

They should change
They? Who?

You, You and You! Every one of you!
You should change, didn't you get the memo?

Oh, no, We didn't
nor did They and Y'all.

In the rush to judgment that is my fate
I count from 2 not 1.

Antidote For Paranoia

Plan for the unexpected
expect the expected.

Fantasy

I am the major-domo of promises
steward of an evanescent menagerie

Promises to keep, I promise . . . but
so many promises made . . .

Keep It Close

All in the family
let's keep it homely

let's speak in homilies
so that no one but us

can understand firmly
as we screw others regularly

not to be mistaken with
ourselves screwing nightly.

Nepotism you say, firmly?
In our firm, we are all family, we say paternally.

Laying Of The Hands—Yours

On the rope of Life
bequeathed, is the first knot
the knot of Self

On the rope of Life
the second knot, the knot you tie
is the Sense of Self.

to know thyself
lay hands on both knots
grasp firmly and always

Loosen your grip on either
loosen your grip on Self and Reality.

*

Laying Of The Feet—Yours

On the rope of Life,
the first knot tied for you
by parent or surrogate
is the knot of Belonging

to belong
plant your feet and
stay rooted to this knot

allow your feet to slip
and you will long to belong.

Unrelenting And Determining

The current of Life, oh so relentless
sweeps us ready or not
kicking and screaming or with equanimity
to the future, nevertheless

Flail or swim, regardless
know this
Destiny is what you make of fate.*
And, fate is happening to you today.

---

*"Destiny is what you make of fate." Reference: Sally Koslow, *Another Side of Paradise: A Novel* (New York: Harper, First Edition, 2018). A quote attributed to the matron of the orphanage in which Sheilah Graham, F. Scott Fitzgerald's last lover, spent her early childhood.

Recasting Perspective

You know me for 40 years, and
my triggers

I know you for 40 years, and
your triggers

We know each other for 40 years
why then, are we triggered?

Oh! So Pavlovian

Expecting an ovation
for every innovation.

Trifecta

Fearless in relationships
fearful of love

my issues, never in denial
in denial of yours

tense about my pretense
pretense about yours

this fearsome trifecta of your reality
pushing our relationship into unreality.

Do I place my bet on your trifecta, or
walk away from the bookie?

Muse: Rodrigo Garcia, *A Farewell to Gabo and Mercedes: A Son's Memoir* (New York: Harpervia, 2021). An intense and insightful account of the final phase in the lives of his parents, Gabriel García Márquez and Mercedes Barcha.

Identity Crisis, Unidentified

My mind, a Hall of Mirrors
where narcissism holds sway

Locked in with multiple images
I pose and gaze back, too enamored

to pose the key question
Who am I, really?

Self-entrapment
Or
Isolation

is a tangled web
we weave
from skeins of
time, space, and
preoccupation.

Voice To Love

Beautiful, graceful, and striking, tattooed arms
holding a phone, speaking animatedly

my senses caught you
as I walked by

my ears, your voice
more than my eyes, your grace

mezzo-soprano, contralto, alto
a sexy drawl I could live with, make love to

I know I can, I did that
to my love, now long gone.

For the length of time it took to stride past you
your voice, my love, caressed me for old times' sake.

Au Naturel

I like my backyard
slummy, slutty, and unkempt
in a tight pas de deux with entropy
threatening a ménage à trois with chaos!

I love plants when they flaunt
a glorious display of blooms
an orgy of color
sticking a finger of disorder into order.

Memories Are Forever . . .

Memories of you are all over my life
your signature all over my memories, Brailled for life

or, so I thought.

As I live Life, and grow wise
I know otherwise

memories are like charcoal drawings.

Fingers of my mind constantly reading you from memory
are smudging the memory tracks, conflating fact and fiction

Are memories forever when Life is Not?

Appearances To Keep

Up. Many, many, many, so many!
Facades more numerous than a Main Street movie lot

Is this the real me, or
the movie-reel me?

Reveal the real me?
Why spoil the show?

I prefer mystery
to my story

Don't know who I am
don't want to know

Playing hide and seek with myself
like many in this world

Now, you see me . . .
no, you didn't, and never will.

Muse: *Keeping Up Appearances* the delightful and oh, so true 1990s BBC series, written by Roy Clarke and starring Patricia Routledge as Hyacinth Bucket (I beg your pardon, Bouquet!).

Makes Sense

A sou
of insouciance
makes one
less intense
and
intestines
less tense

Makes sense.

Revelation

You leave no stone unturned
every shortcoming of mine
turned over and hurled at me

scab that forms
guaranteed to re-bleed
a meddler, scratcher, and miscellaneous excoriator

of my self and confidence.
why then do I live with you?
are you a proxy for self-harm of my soul?

Bipolar Vocabulary

Amaaazing! Distressing!
Careening from one to the other and nothing in-between

Mind-blowing! Mind-numbing!
Frozen in a thought desert

Heart overflowing! Heartbroken!
Blood on the floor, slipping and sliding to extremes

Love You! Hate You!
Emotions on a yo-yo

Emoting in an adjective bubble
while living in reality

Polar nature of a binary life
polarizing to the extreme

An exclamatory life
Oh, so draining for self and the other.

Then And Now

In the beginning . . .
relationship in a tight embrace
nightly race to a dreamless sleep
spooned and almost aswoon

Two-score years later . . .
spoons, spoon no more
one, flashes hot and cold, like a firefly in the night
the other, freezer cold.

Then, hormones in holy matrimony conjoining us
Till Death Do Us Apart
Now, hormones in unholy disharmony
Heat Makes Us Sleep Apart.

Life Cycles

There they stood
in front of all that wood
some still rooted in trees that stood
others routed to their house in the woods

Radiant she and ebullient he
in their finery
posing for posterity
someone else's past as backdrop scenery

Full of hope for a new life that waited
while new life incubated
some in her womb
some still a glint in the parents' eyes

There stood all that wood
present witness to family life cycle beginning, and
past witness to the home builders
family life cycle ending

There they stood
in front of all that wood
breathing new life into the house
where once someone else stood.

Dedicated to individuals starting on a cycle of life.

Behold! I Flow!

I am a woman and I flow
monthly, mostly

I am a woman and I cramp
monthly, mightily

I am a woman and I bloat
monthly, mostly,

I am a woman and I may
get moody, monthly

I am a woman and I flow
with the flow of being a woman

while I flow
monthly, mostly.

Now, if men did flow like women flow
there would be peace on Earth, mostly.

Relationships, Require Relating

I will tell you my expectations
and, you tell me yours

Tell me what turns you on
and, I will tell you, in turn
for mutual turn on

Tell me what turns you off
and, I will tell you, in turn
for mutual resolution, in time

Tell me what you want
and I will tell you, if I can meet that want

If you do not tell me what you desire
I cannot give you what you want

If you do tell me what you desire
I may not give you what you want

If I cannot give you what you want
I can give you what I can

If you can take what I give
you know what I cannot give

Tell me what you expect in a relationship
not what you think I can give.

Muse: Dancer and friend, SSM.

On My Way Out[†]

Your Life boat is sliding down
the slip of Life into Oblivion

I live on
memories of you in a tight hug

*

Departure draws nigh
the thought makes me sigh

not because I am leaving
but because you left me

I wave goodbye to you
through my memories

*

On my way out of your empty
and shuttered house
I pause

at the soon to be shut front door
look back one last time
and, lock

in my memory
my love for you . . . and
discard the key.

†Read the poems on page 42-49 in tandem.

Muse: Harbinder Kaur Chatta, 79 years young, died June 2013. I liked and respected the way she lived life after her husband's death; she told me, and I agree, that the void left by the passing of a loved one remains and memories are permanent, and it does not stop her from living life to the fullest.

S's poem*

The markets and parks
around your house
I knew them all
C-Block market
D-Block market
A-Block park
this "Vihar" and that "Bagh"
I knew them all
pulsating with life
in spite of tripe of every stripe.

I knew the
byways
alleyways
all ways
always, the quickest way.

I knew them
and
they, me
because
I knew you—Dadi.

Now
that you are gone from this Life
I will do what you did so well,

square my shoulders
stand erect, in body, mind and soul
and navigate
the alleyways
of my life.

C-Block market
D-Block market
A-Block park
this "Vihar" and that "Bagh"
You taught me your Life Lessons
Just as Dadi taught me hers:
fixate on living, not the hearse.

*Read the poems on page 42-49 in tandem.

S, my muse, deferred her college admission by a year to be in India with her terminally ill, paternal grandmother.

Memory—Trick Or Treat?*

Analgesia
of amnesia
yields
nostalgia.

*Read the poems on page 42-49 in tandem.

Arrival Equals Departure*

Visited your empty house.

Can sense your essence
but, sans your physical presence
arrival equals departure.

*Read the poems on page 42-49 in tandem.

Morning Ritual*

of tea, biscuits, newspaper
and
friendship
a staple
of our lives.

Dollop of laughter
dash of gossip
talk of family, friends and enemies
all in the mix.

Now, just as you
no more.

*Read the poems on page 42-49 in tandem.

Mummy's Recipe Book*

Opened it today
to make her green bean dish

my hands brushed
over her neat hand

fingers rubbing over
burnishing memories

of watching her cook
learning her ways

calling her—across time zones
Ma! tell me!
How do I cook this—sauté that?

Mummy's recipe book
my Ouija board.

*Read the poems on page 42-49 in tandem.

Double-Speak

You speak Truth To The People,
lies to me

A Savior Of The People
destroyer of us the couple

People, Lose Not Hope you urge
our love you purge

Long before you Wed The People
you wed me

Living in alternate realities, we live the sham of marriage
for what would The People say

Once more declaring ourselves
man and wife

we walk down the aisle
to make our vows to infidelity.

Dedicated to those who break free of toxic relationships.

Ardent Lover

I love you as always
in the absence of pretense
here, there and everywhere.

Call It As It Is

Awesome
Fantastic
Excellent

overused, and threadbare of meaning.

Awesome
Fantastic
Excellent

are best reserved for

awesome
fantastic, and
excellent things—rare instances
of otherworldliness.

May I suggest,
Okay
Good
Ordinary, for

okay
good, and
ordinary things?

And, even

unimpressive
inferior, when it is so?

Incoming

will keep coming
you cannot bind the inbound

barricade mightily
evade diligently

external influences will reach you, pierce you
no matter what you do

the external world corrupts and enlightens
from time of humanity on Earth, probably before that too

the challenge for you, me and all sundry
how to influence the influence and control the influence

exert mightily
persevere diligently

discarding dross and dregs
expanding education and enlightenment.

Promissory
Or
Pro-misery

I said, am going my way

You said, will follow my way

till your dying day.

On my way, I look back

running my way, is a promise

running on empty.

Muse: Poet, songwriter, and singer extraordinaire, Leonard Cohen's poem, "The sweetest little song" from his collection, *Book of Longing* (New York: Ecco Press, 2006).

My World View
Or
Delusions Of Grandeur

My world view says you are wrong
My world view says you are stupid
My world view says you have no view of the world

Have I considered that my world view is my world view?

And that, maybe . . . is there a chance . . . could it be

that neither, My world view is The World's view
nor, is there one.

Muse: Florence Luscomb, architect and suffragist (1887-1985). Reference: A.Word.A.Day with Anu Garg, February 6, 2017, https://wordsmith.org/awad/archives/0217.

The Resentment

The work I do for you
is more than the work
you do for me

Do you ask for parity?
Of course not! You guess, holding onto broigus*
Thus, resending your resentment in an infinite loop.

*Broigus, a Yiddish word that roughly translates to a deep and abiding resentment for another person because of some long-standing grievance which the other is unaware of.

I Watched

as you held me fiercely
and, kissed passionately

You treat me with respect.

I watched
as you verbally abused a waiter
about lukewarm coffee.

You treat others with no respect!

Rage was evident,
source was not.

Who are you lover?
Love of my Life
or
future killer of my Soul?

The Guilt Of Conscience

weighs a ton
wanton thoughts
of sliding into hellfire and brimstone

I step closer to the grate
unintended consequences of my action
the unfastened trapdoor.

Self-Farmer

I am a dedicated farmer
farming my self, tending to my growth
before pulling weeds from my partner's field

making the time
never forced
patient, persistent, and persevering.

Conflate not navel-gazing and self-farming
one, aspires to inflate ideal undeliverables
the other, inspires with deliverables.

Savior, Heed This

Thunder roared
rain poured
gutters thundered
pumps surrendered

Water crept up
lapped over the fenders, engine died
my car is going under

You splashed by in a truck, stretched out your hand to help
My Savior!
Deposited in my outstretched hand, four—read that—four
spark plugs! And, drove away
leaving me in your wake, as I watched your tow hitch recede
along with you.

Do what you need to do before you do what you want to do.

Dedicated to people who receive inappropriate aid.

Not This Time*

Back in the land of the living
walking the paths
familiar from a year ago.

The only change to you, is my smooth
perfectly symmetrical, post-chemotherapy, bald head
irresistibly inviting to the passerby.

Looks so smooth and shiny
like a billiard ball
can I touch it, feel it?

You are touching, you are feeling
a different person
than who walked these paths before.

I know now, what I did not earlier—
we are numbers on the roulette wheel of Death
spun by the hand of Luck

the ball of Chance, all smooth and shiny
can fall into my slot at any time, only this time, it didn't
and I was a Winner, in spite of losing!

*Read this poem and the next in tandem.

Muse: KH, a Master's Program student who had to abruptly discontinue studies to undergo major cancer surgery. She successfully fought-off cancer, rejoined the Program, and graduated.

STOP!*

I am done!
Free!
Don't ask me, "Are you well?"

I am well! Thank you!

I am grateful for your concern
you supported me every step of the way
as I crawled back to Life!

I can never re-pay your kindness!

But now, you must STOP!
Stop enquiring about my health
Ask me about Life

Enquire about my Love Life!

My Work Life!
Any Life!
Not my health!

I want to savor Life, while I have it.

*Read the previous poem and this in tandem.

Yellow, The Warm Color Of Love

morning light on my bed
cascading through the windows

draping my undressed body
in a diaphanous, yellow sundress

warm and enveloping embrace from afar
surrogate and reminder of your love, My Love.

Healing Can't Come Fast Enough

In time
I will be well
healed

In the meantime
the Tincture of Time is
bitter.

Utopian Dream—Dystopian Reality*

Tire scrunches over trigger
contact switch closes
bare-bones circuitry fails
roadside bomb remains intact
so do my Soldier Brothers—My Dream.

Sudden blackness
pitiless dismemberment
I am left, scraping remains
scrapping with dogs
scouring for remains—My Reality.

Sorry, My Brothers
I could not save you.
The blame is not mine
but I mine the blame
for nuggets to cherish.

*Read this poem and the next in tandem.

Muse: Iraq War veteran Michael Pitre, and his vivid work of fiction about that war *Fives and Twenty-Fives. A Novel* (New York: Bloomsbury USA, an imprint of Bloomsbury Publishing Plc, 2014).

Utopian Dream—Dystopian Reality, Revisited*

My Dream, My Reality
My Reality, My Dream
Reality became my Dream

Wandering in my dreamscape with no escape
trying to escape back to reality
I tried and tested every fad including FAD

Firewater—Aggression—Drugs
to drown, and kill
Sorrow and Guilt

Sorrow and Guilt
would not drown or be killed
unlike My Brothers

About to close the Death Switch
and fulfill my Death Wish to join My Brothers
laid low by my own hand, unlike My Brothers

you chanced upon me
saw in me, what I did not see
felt in me, what I did not feel

Diminutive in body, colossus in spirit and spunk
you returned the esprit de corps to my soul
spirited away when My Brothers became Spirits

Your constant presence in my life
eyes wide open view of the world
quiet voice, ability to enjoy the moment, and honesty

became the sluice gate to my dammed sorrow
the bartender to my bottled guilt
You opened the gate, and uncorked the bottle

War memories of pain, death, and loss
poured out of me in your presence
unflinching and bereft of emotion, you listened

In time, and with your time, I returned to the Land of the Living.
Dreams of the past continue to escape into Reality, but now,
I have you . . . my dreamcatcher.

*Read the previous poem and this in tandem.

Non

No Heart
No Art!

Archivist Or Arsonist—A Choice

In the library of my lived experience
I am the archivist, cataloging and annotating memories
to identify and hold the hot cups of tea

helps me stay moist and wet not only in the eye
in nooks and crannies
for things that call for moistness and wetness

keeps me warm and dry not only on the skin
in my heart and mind
for things that call for warmth and objectivity.

In the library of my lived experience
I am the librarian, identifying elephants in the room
consciously, consistently.

In the library of our lived experience
we are librarians, to one another
researching issues, lending experiences.

A relationship that works
is a fusion of lived experiences
there is so much that happened, we don't know about

be both archivist and librarian to self and other
else, it will burn like Constantinople's Imperial Library, or
wither from neglect like the Libraries of Alexandria.

Yet Again*

The dark side of the moon
where communication ceases

You are inexplicably, yet again
on the dark side of our relationship

Are we still on the good ship, Made for One Another
bound for the distant star, Matrimony?

You do not answer
radio silence greets my query

My question diminishes
to nothingness

held incommunicado
in a vacuum of silence

You trap yourself, on your way
to our mailbox

Caught in the existential bear trap
of the here and now

The eternal, bird in hand
is better than a bird in the bush

(Matters little to you, that
I am a bird in the bank)

Playing at the Relationship Casino
with chips from a current Lover

Silly you, our relationship is never on the table
to be gambled, pawned or bartered

I'm available to be invited
. . . yet again.

*Read this poem and the next in tandem.

Both poems highlight the importance of communication and having similar core values for the survival and deepening of a relationship, and also, the danger of staying in a dysfunctional one.

Inviting The Uninvited*

Oh, the shame!

I do know you possess me

I do not know what possesses me

to not possess you!

Oh, the shame!

A Lover In Hand

is all I need . . .

as I run unfettered through Life.

But, I love you so . . .

Oh, the shame!

A Lover in Hand

is all I need . . .

not a possession . . . for now.

*Read the previous poem and this in tandem.

Fat Head

neither good
for the head
nor
will get you
ahead.

Muse: A conversation with longtime friend, JoC.

Early Morning Memories

Many suns ago, my Sun still rising

I see a beloved figure

seated on the bed's edge, slightly hunched

neatly dressed, hair in a tight bun

Fingers held in apposition, tightly

pressed on the chin, firmly

tips reaching the lips, nearly

fixed gaze, focused on infinity

faraway look—classic—do not disturb

Thoughts, she said, when asked,

Avaya, what are you thinking?

Childhood, parents, parenthood, children

Thoughts!

Avatar, visiting a long gone, time and space

inhabited by memories, jostling for her attention

bidding them a pleasant morning, in a place with no morning

attempting to be an equal opportunity sampler.

Many suns later, my Sun in summer solstice

a pleasant apparition—Avaya—long gone, grandmother.

Indulge Not Bulge

Cannolo
is yummy.
Cannoli
is tummy!

The Public Phone Booth

Our relationship needs a phone booth

a private place in a public space

to stimulate moistness in our pubic space

we need that enclosed place as we live our lives

to make space for our needs and each other.

We don't need to feed the slot with quarters to gain access

the call is free to our mind and body

when our mind and body awaits to access the other.

Muse: The disappearing public pay phone booth, once ubiquitous in cities, which required feeding a slot with quarters (coins) to call. Reference: NPR, "Last call: New York City bids an official farewell to its last public pay phone," 2022, https://www.npr.org/2022/05/24/1100931534/last-pay-phone-new-york-city-public-nyc.

Older ≠ Wiser

Cross-ventilate

your mind
is a living thing

open the windows
leave the door ajar

like dust
wisdom accrues with age

like dust
alive

with mites of experience
each, with a mote of knowledge

all together, a kingdom
of syncretic wisdom

but, all is lost
if you shut your mind

you will preside
over wizened thoughts

crumbling into sterile dust.

Muse: Lyme Disease research scientist MP's phrase
. . . but bacteria may enter a mind left ajar!

Control The Troll—I & II

Control the urge
to control.

Control

generates vitriol
and,
vitiates control.

No Buyer's Remorse

Best to . . .

obambulate
perambulate
circumambulate

through your choices
before you decide

Not after.

The Unified States Of Orgasm

Orgasm is thunderous

more than a local spasm, when

Northern sensation mates with Southern engorgement

guided by, bi-Coastal manual dexterity.

> Muse: Gendun Chopel, *The Passion Book: A Tibetan Guide to Love and Sex*, translated by Donald S. Lopez, Jr., and Thupten Jinpa (Chicago: The University of Chicago Press, 2018). Completed in the 1930's, this book of verse is an insightful and detailed commentary on love, sex, and relationships, based on scholarship and personal experience.

Empathy For Realists

I am happy to see
that you see and feel what you think I see and feel

and am secure in the truth
that you see and feel what I do not.

You, in turn, are content that I see and feel what you do not
We know, we cannot

unless,
we become the other.

A Mentor

untested
by Life
is a
mentee-in-waiting.

Am I Your Friend?

I didn't get in . . .
did you?

I hope you didn't . . .

No, that's silly
you are my friend

And, I want the best
for my friends . . .

Do I?

Duality—a quality of humanity
is a reality
accept it

And, yes!
I am still, your friend!

Love In Three Acts

Love her
Lover
Leave her

NOT!

From the top, once more

Love her
Lover
Live with her

Forever.

Two Questions For Spouses

Did the beliefs
you espoused
change after you espoused
your spouse?

And,

Did the spice in your life
before you espoused
disappear when spouse
appeared?

Liquor As Metaphor

Highballs are good
Cocktails even better
But at times
I like it missionary straight.

Did It Happen?

I kissed you
on the forehead
while you slept.

Does that count
as a mark of my love
for you, my love?

Did the plant bloom
if no one witnessed
the blooming plant?

Rain, The Great Motivator

Lying in bed
bound by lassitude
frustrated by slow recovery
from major surgery
listening to rain on the metal roof
the staccato cadence
hammering in my head,
echoing the commands of the drill sergeant
resident in my mind:
Listen up—Straighten up—Get the fuck up!

Resolute inability, meet immutable resolve.

Muse: AL, veterinary pathologist, excellent research scientist, and visionary. He lived in a metal roofed house, not uncommon in hurricane-prone Louisiana. He liked the poem and felt it captured his state of mind post-surgery. Sadly, he lost his life in mortal combat with cancer.

Gender Discrimination Need Not Apply

Employer
employ Her
Them
All.

Anticipatory Anxiety

In the waiting room
waiting for the doctor
to pronounce me dead!
Sudden sharp pain in my chest
brought me here.

Localized,
costochondral junction
waxing and waning
with respiration
can point to it.

Aha! Says my training
Costochondritis!
One of the differentials for
sudden pain in the chest.
Symptomatic treatment
and, good to go.

Could be . . .
but wait,
here comes my *id* . . . with the death knell.

Lytic lesion—rib
I can almost hear
the doctor pronounce, gravely.

Ah-ha! Says my training
when you hear hooves
think horses not zebras!
May be . . .
my *id* thinks otherwise
could be zebras this time.

But wait,
here comes a damsel
to my distress . . .
my wife, also an M.D.,

She takes one look,
and pronounces me
"alive, with a tinge of self-indulgent
impending doom."

A 15 Minute Hug

is what we need
to transfer
mutual love, respect
and
caring.

A parabiosis* of souls.

What I get
is a shrug,
and a tug
of the welcome rug
from under
our relationship.

* Artificial joining of two bodies.

Noblesse Oblige

these days
neither noble
nor an obligation
Merely a notion
that good is done
as a means to an end—
resumé padding and tax sinks, anyone?

Interns' Lament

—not easy to be patient
when neither resident nor patient
shows patience.

Residents' rejoinder—
reside as we do with our patients
and in time your patience
will not reside with you!

Patients' respond—
interns in turn become patients
to see what becomes of your patience!

Life's inexorable lesson—
interns, lament not
In time, you will become
both residents and patients.

Knowledge

is a wedge
with a sharp edge.

In unwieldy hands
easy to split humankind
into
haves
and
have-nots.

Self-help With No Help

Get off
your tush
to push
through Life
In spite of Life
pushing right back.

Wanderlust

I wander
down under and all around

inland, island, all manner of lands
a traveler through towns

names so outlandish
tongue in a perpetual twist

a life encumbered by suitcases
and no other baggage

room to room
room for occasional friend or lover

solitary and unafraid existence
filled with experiences

wanderlust occupies my mind
lest my unhappiness does.

Thanksgiving

Such soft hands
sign that I haven't held them enough

Such soft cheeks
sign that I haven't kissed them enough

Such a soft voice
I never tire of hearing it enough

Happy and optimistic
except when I anger you enough

Enough is enough, I better get going
our time together is never enough.

Fantasy Or Reality

We don't ask
we imagine.

Imagine
a synonym for fantasy

fans of the easy way out
in control of our fantasies

we loosen at inopportune moments
our grip on the opportunity of reality.

Inheritance

Humans fight over property
we do not own

money we did not earn
things we did not acquire

in many cases, multi-generational property
of unknown provenance.

Tense over inheritance
siblings fight and inherit tenseness

laden with the curses of
similarly incensed ancestors.

Selective Resiliency

Artists given a chance
paint with any material
coffee, tea, pigment of all origins and hew

Making masterpieces anew

Why then
do we humans fight one another
over pigment, origin, and anything new?

Delayed Union

I, an *in silico* stud
romantic algorithm yielding null

you, Goddess in a gynecoid pelvis
troubled mind wielding a sexy body

we, lost one another
in the fog bank of our future

emerging five decades later
from the bog of sucking relationships

covered in toxic slime
of lies and accusations

we fell into one another's arms
two lost souls reuniting with the soul we lost.

Anchored Friends

Some friends of yore
ship their oars*
drop anchor on a version of me
that exists no more

not understanding
or willing to understand
or open to understanding
making no motion of their own

that my past version
is not a permanent stand-in
for the present, which
bears little relation to the past

they drag anchor and
our friendship drags
on same old, same old perceptions
of a past that plays out in their reality

Anchored friends
don't you see
my Life Boat is named
Version 3?

Ship oars: To stop rowing and pull the oars inside or alongside the boat. Reference: Trout Unlimited, "A new way to ship your oars," 2021, https://www.tu.org/magazine/fishing/boats/quick-tip-a-new-way-to-ship-your-oars/.

The Tension

If focused, I am an idiot savant
If broad in interests
I am an unfocused 'gasp' generalist
Is there relief from this tension?

Focused and generalist
can they co-exist?
The answer is hidden in time
the time I make not the time I take

to live in my three marriages*
marriage to work
marriage to self
marriage to other.

---

*The poet and author David Whyte coined the term "Three Marriages" in his book, *The Three Marriages: Reimagining Work, Self and Relationship* (New York: Riverhead Books, Reprint edition, 2010). (Footnote continues on page 109.)

Bin There—Dun That

nothing more to discover
is when you die
'til then
'tis always
being here—doing this
discovering new things
in yourself and the world.

The concept of three marriages describes something that all of us already live in.
To reiterate and paraphrase David Whyte, we are in three marriages. And, each may have sub-marriages.
- Marriage to other. The "other" is partner, parents, siblings, children, family, friends, group, volunteer organization, community, nation etc.
- Marriage to work. "Work" refers not only to employment, but also, the work of a homemaker outside of child-rearing. Your passion qualifies, too.
- Marriage to self. Looking after self in all manner of small and large ways. Sleep and nutrition matter. Self-reflection, oft ignored, is crucial.

These three marriages, in theory, are separate lives, but in practice are more like a dynamic Venn diagram and are in constant tension with one another. There is no work-life balance.

I added this rider, "Daily, or at times hourly, these marriages are re-prioritized, and as long as there is communication and cooperation between people in these three marriages, we manage quite well."

Shakti—*Almost*

Female of our species

Force of Life

yes, you are
a pillar of strength
an anchor of Life
a bearer of arms
legs, brain and all else.

Without you
I wouldn't be here
nor the rest of humanity

In Good Faith

It is said
God gives burdens, also shoulders
easy to say, not shoulder
burdens are unequal
some easier to shoulder
boulders require more than a pair of shoulders.

Muse: A German proverb. Reference: Commentary, "Burdens, Shoulders, and President Carter," 1983, https://www.commentary.org/articles/reader-letters/burdens-shoulders-and-president-carter/.

Teen Daymare

At the beach
no one within reach

ogling women in bikinis
all out of reach

stoked on hormones
on a libido high

feeling wet
not from the water nigh

a veteran of wet dreams
I fancy myself an expert

on all things, breasts
specializing in pert

consultant with no street cred
I expound with foot in mouth

wired versus non-wired
molded cup for pert or not.

Fired-up with bravado, I try a pickup line
I sidle up to a woman in an un-wired bra

"Can you make an exception
I have horrible Wi-Fi reception

can I stand next to your wireless, and
hope for better reception?"

Reality does not deliver
what we prefer

It delivered instead
two slaps with a slipper

Living my teen daymare
I open my mouth to change feet.

Clarity Of Distance

On an island beach
far from public reach

solitude cleaning my soul
like gentle waves washing sand

thoughts obscured by the fog of contentious proximity
re-emerge with the clarity of distance

a transactional union for years and years
tears and tears over many years

bitter arguments filled our ears
then bisection and disunion within a year

like trade winds carrying odors from afar
and ocean currents floating jetsam away

our current actions carry downstream to the future
influencing deeds with forgotten origins.

Ability

is a function of Time, Space and Resources

Give an able human all three opportunities

watch ability expand to infinity.

The Organized Person

Bags shoulder to shoulder
color distinct from its neighbor
suspended in pairs by dowels
spanning the shopping cart

Perfect posture, focused countenance
pressed button-down shirt all prim and proper
typed and categorized list on blue clipboard
pen at the ready to cross off items on the list

greens in green
fruits in yellow
dry goods in brown, and
wet in dry bag

fastidiously placed in particular bags
no doubt preordained by list
items in bags
no items left to cross on the list.

Dear Organized Person
how are you doing
with organizing your lovers and others
in the image of your person?

When you fail to organize others
take heart in this insight
your mind and organs are organized
not your digestion.

Know Thyself

You smile and laugh a lot
undoubtedly, I do

you appear happy a ton
did you have some "weed" seed?

indeed, by the ton
not weed or seed

you are stimulated endlessly
are you on stimulants?

if you say so
I am not in control of your perceptions

My secret, you ask?
Myself.

What I Really Need Is—

—a partner who listens
to me
as I listen
to them

—a person who cares about me
not as a sex object
as someone they love and respect
as I do about them

—a human who sees me
as an equal
no less
no more than I see them

—a lover who gazes at my body
with all its imperfections of which there are many
and hunger for mine
as I salivate for theirs

—an intelligent soul
who recognizes
a kindred spirit
in mine

—an equal laborer
at home
so that
I don't labor alone

—a person who brings home the bacon
in turn
appreciates
when I bring it home, alone

—a teacher
who does not patronize
a student
who does not condescend

*

Instead, I got a
lousy, lily-livered, loutish lay about
lusting after leftover lovers.

Sadly, we are two more
I am walking away from you
not from our two

I will do unto them
what we should have
done unto us.

Know This

Kids and adults petition against repetition
'oh, the perdition of repetition,' we moan

seeing no more than
the dull metronome

forgetting the life-giving
repetition of sunrise

repetition is inbuilt in Nature
until she shrugs shoulders

repetition is built into our lives
until we die, maybe in the hereafter too

maybe time
to recast perspective with data.

Not In Any Dictionary

Our relationship
unformalized in form
far from the formalized norm
that pervades society

Therein lies its charm!

Muse: An email exchange with old colleague DDR about pithy words in regional South Asian languages that defy dictionary meanings.

Partner In Absentia

Gone for a few days on business
I look for you in the usual places

I set the table for two
when there was one

is this love
or is it habit?

if it is habit
is there no love?

is it habit and love
or another form of

she loves me
she loves me not

some form of insecurity
when there should be none.

I walked our daily route late at night
to the accompaniment of questions

by friendly neighbors out walking their dogs
Where is your hand-holding partner?

Are they acknowledging our love or our habit? Or both?

Does it matter? Isn't this mindless chatter when love is a biological habit?

Keep It Simple

I love you
you love me

yet, here we are in Confounder Hell
a deep pit we dug ourselves into

smearing one another with slander
watching our relationship flounder

is it too late to keep it simple
refocus on first principles

I love you
you love me.

Matter Of Course

Visiting friends and relatives

amidst all the discourses

partaking in many courses

is of course

par for the course.

Eyes Tell No Lies

I stand and watch
my child's union to their chosen

just as my parents watched
my arranged union to an unchosen

a child born out of a loveless union
exposed only to the love of a single parent

and the love of many self-appointed
honorary grand parents

now sprinkled throughout the
watching throng.

I stand and watch unseeing
the happy scene unfolding

mind fixed on a wistful dream horizon
where dreams come true

eyes fail to comply
eyes tell no lies

seeing only the long journey
the strife and the pain

my face follows suit
mirroring the journey

eyes and face forever captured
in the record of a happy day.

Ask Not Guess

there is no holding back
humans pass gas
easily

we guess
like we pass gas
easily

we don't ask
like we pass gas
easily

if we asked more than we guessed
our relationships wouldn't stink
easily.

China Syndrome*
AKA
Law Of Unintended Consequences

Secretive types
secrete emotions
in secret
spaces of the mind.

Secure in the knowledge
that the secrets are secure
from the prying eyes
of the world.

Little realizing that
emotions by definition
are wiggly creatures, constantly
seeking freedom from serfdom!

---

*China syndrome a hypothetical sequence of events following the meltdown of a nuclear reactor, in which the core melts through its containment structure and deep into the earth. Origin 1970s: from China (as being on the opposite side of the earth from a reactor in the US)—New Oxford American Dictionary.

Virality Of Fantasy

In the bedroom of your mind
pay no fealty to reality

skinny-dip in unreality
engage with your physicality

let the virality of fantasy
infect your sexuality, and

enjoy fleeting power over reality
as you climax in actuality.

Love Me . . .

. . . but not as a chore to do.

We don't have to do
what we thought
we would do
if our minds
are busy
with other things to do.

I need your mind
to be clear and calm
and
not thinking
of chores to do.

I am your lover
not a whore
with a chore to do.

Simplicate, And Then Add Lightness*

a beautiful concept
worthy of actualization.

Readily applicable
to complicated
and
inanimate
cars.

Readily inapplicable
to complicated
and
animate
beings.

*Phrase co-opted by the late Colin Chapman, founder, Lotus Engineering Ltd., the original manufacturer of Lotus cars; relates to his design philosophy when building sports and racing cars. Original phrase variously attributed to the inventor William Bushnell Stout and his designer, Gordon Hooton. Reference: Wikipedia, "William Bushnell Stout," 2024, https://en.wikipedia.org/wiki/William_Bushnell_Stout.

Temptation Of Rationality

Just this once
may work
if
just is once
but
just, is never once.

Depression

is an oppression
that knows no suppression
if you try to suppress
what oppresses.

A Suite For Suitors

Suitor

neither wear a suit
nor be tutored.
Keep it simple
you
need to
suit her.

Suitor Of Other Genders

engender competition
at your own risk
for what is sauce for the goose
is sauce for the gander!

Suitor Of Any Gender

neither wear a suit
nor be tutored.
As luck may have it
you may end up
with a tutored Suit.*

---

*Suit: Slang for manager or authority figure. Reference: Urban Dictionary, 2003, https://www.urbandictionary.com/define.php?term=suit.

Backed Up

I trap my crap
lower the trap
into the depths of my being

reverse of a crab-trapper
I don't raise traps
to examine my crap

hard-wired for compartmentalization
lacking self-reflection
lucid moments tell me

take a crap
expel long-suppressed accumulations
backed-up into concretions of misery

could
should
cannot.

Cohabitants!

Habitation extends
beyond the bed.

To ensure
habitation continues
as cohabitation discontinues

splurge on the urge to wed
once the urgency
to surge and plunge
has ebbed.

Authority Figures
(calling all parents and coaches)

figure this:
parenting and coaching protégés
sans their copayment
in time and effort,
will ensure
pay the rent—parents
who
co–ache with the coaches.

Marriageable Age

why should my reproductive capacity
determine my marriageability?

am I a cow in a country fair
looking for a stud bull in the winner's circle?

don't answer, I know
belief, society, peers, family . . . primordial urge

urging me to be in the family way
en famille along the way

I get that
I don't seek that

Get that?

The company has fallen into chaos since you were absent. Unlike other companies, I will never let you go.*

How Nice

    to receive
    a note of thanks
    and
    a vote of confidence
    from a boss
    who knows
    your loss
    is not only
    your loss.

*Attributed to Motoo Matsuura, President, Juken Kogyo. Reference: Takehiko Kambayashi, "In Japan, better with age," *Christian Science Monitor Weekly*, volume 104, issue 41, September 2, 2012, page 30.

Show Me, In The Light

Make love to me with the lights on
not in the dark

I want to see
as I feel you

Let's celebrate our love
in the light

See my naked body
show me, yours

I revel in my naked self
as I reveal myself in the light

I have nothing to hide from you
in body or mind

What are you hiding, and why?
If you cannot reveal your body, how can you, your mind?

Way It Is, Always

The way things were
are never the way things are
in the past, present or future.

No Strings Attached

Puppeteer of my dreams
jerking my emotions and desires
like you own them

going to places in my mind I never did go
planting thoughts I never had
shadow burglar in reverse
implanting false memories

I love what's between your legs
not what's between your ears
I see through you and still like the show

Before I am fucked up beyond all repair
I need to hustle, show some mental muscle
cut the strings, stop being a marionette, and

star in my own one run,
many acts,
mono act.

Habit Forming Humans

Consciously mendacious
and
unconsciously mendacious

two states of lying
separated
by practice.

Indigent Get It, Don't Patronize

Folks who have none of less
in power no less
rarely speak truth to the people
who have more of none

Savior complex to the fore
hope should be offered more and more
Sounds reasonable they say
for without hope, hope is no more.

Self-inflicted guilt to the fore
about their good fortune more and more
let's extend hope for the poor
for we have nothing more.

Speak truth to the people
the masses, especially the poor get it
they understand profit and loss
always did

their world which is not yours
is finely tuned unlike yours
where profit and loss are often synonyms for
life and death.

Unmoved

waiting for your move
wrap me in your arms
show me you care

islands move
continents do too
not you.

Let Sleeping Dogs Lie*

Don't look back
something might be gaining on you
said Satchel Paige.

As I age
I look back at my life arc
and see

the pendulum of life
swings
back and forth

blind to virtue
or
absence thereof

in the long-term
in the end
perchance it all evens out

a matter of chance
after a certain point.

---

*Read this and the next poem in tandem.

Muse: Satchel Paige, the very quotable and evergreen baseball legend. Reference: Quote Investigator, "Don't look back. Something might be gaining on you," 2020, https://quoteinvestigator.com/2020/11/02/gaining/.

Let Sleeping Dogs Lie, Again*

Know thy future
foreknowledge forecloses on failure
say the soothsayers

It's all in the stars
Virgo is in your house, act now
say the astrologers

Ergo the large numbers
who act or not
by the stars.

Let's pretend I can portend
wouldn't it be nice to foretell my future?
"This is where my career-arc will take me!"

Would I like to know what I don't?
Yes, when it comes to knowledge, but foreknowledge?
So many questions with no answers

Let's still pretend I can portend and read the tea leaves
Would the absence of murky tea obscuring the leaves
pluck from my path any chance of finding two leaves and a bud?

No serendipity? That would be a pity.
No pathway to explore? What a bore.
No rabbit hole to dive into? No rabbit in that hole.

Know not thy future
foreknowledge forecloses on initiative
says my intuition.

*Read the previous poem and this in tandem.

Crowd Control

Louisianans
in the lower latitudes
have a history of servitude
to the crawfish multitude!

Louisiana—Revisited

Lower the latitude
Better the attitude.

Single

Leave me alone
I'm one, with myself
Thank you!

Universality Of Energy

When I'm busy and engaged with something, I'm no longer bothered
That's blather! You can be idle and disengaged and still feel badgered

we conflate busy with activity, physical or otherwise
I blame the mash-up on adages by sages

"an idle mind is the Devil's workshop"
"meditation is good for nothing"

give the Devil his due, he was not idle
he sidled into your active mind long before it dawdled, and

being quiet and doing nothing
is also being busy and engaged

quiet and disengaged are acts of activity not passivity
all states of emotion require an active process—energy

so, be busy and engaged
being quiet, doing nothing and no longer bothered

in synergy
with energy.

Muse: A conversation with USM; close friend and good human.

Moving Blues

Movers groaning
Children moaning
Dog groveling
Parents growling
Altogether now,
it could be worse
Let's have some grinning and moving!

NASDeC*

Keep your eyes on her eyes
she is your assistant, here to work, not your wife

counsel your base instincts, let not your peter rise, and watch your stock rise, in her eyes.

*Nubile assistant showing deep cleavage.

The Undoing

I am not what I have done, said he
what you have done, is just not done, and now
you have undone what was done between us, said she

can we redo what was undone?
I cannot undo what was done, said he
another love done gone, said she.

Muse: "I am not what I have done" is a quote by the protagonist during a post-screening discussion about the documentary "Stranger at Home," which chronicles his journey and that of his wife and family while combating PTSD. This is a searing, searching, and must-see film about the armed forces and the stigma around mental health that the world needs to see. Information about the movie: Stranger At Home, 2023, https://strangerathome.org.

Cancer

can
certainly
kill.

★

Cancer

untrammeled,
trammels
Life.

Multiple Personalities And Counting

When I meet you
and you meet me
we are not two but six

two for how we see ourselves
two for how we see one another
two for how we really are

thus spoke Dr. Oliver Wendell Holmes Sr.*
I hazard the good doctor misspoke the count
six and counting

for how we really are, are many fleeting avatars
depending on age, mood, and station in life
manifestations that manifest as we flit through reality.

---

*References: Oliver Wendell Holmes, *The Autocrat of the Breakfast Table*, Chapter 3 (1858). A collection of essays published in book form. First published as essays in monthly installments starting with the first issue of *Atlantic Monthly* in late 1857 (https://www.ibiblio.org/eldritch/owh/abt03.html). The physician, poet, and polymath writes on the human condition in a delightful, humorous, and utterly insightful way.
William James, *The Principles of Psychology*, Chapter X, The Consciousness of Self (New York: Henry Holt and Company, 1890).

Undeliverable

Unsinnable, unsinkable
conformable, always able

Unable to make such humans
available.

Worth Or The Absence Thereof

I know what I will lose
when we lose ourselves

Do you?

Muse #1: Alenka Artnik the Slovenian free diver. The fantastic story of her life and exploits is presented in unique fashion by the story studio Long Lead. Reference: LongLead.com, "The Depths She'll Reach," 2021, https://onjustonebreath.com.
Muse #2: Antonio Porchia the Italian-born Argentinian poet's famous poem which appears in the introductory note by the translator of his collection. Reference: Antonio Porchia, *Voices*, translated by W.S. Merwin (Port Townsend, USA: Copper Canyon Press, 2003).

First Day
(at a new job)

is not your best day.
Uprooted and muted,
your public persona
is incognito
amongst the
strange cognoscenti.

Humanity's Essence*

You toiled and boiled for others
were cut and bled by others
while you cut to heal others

You loved and lost,
found and lost
all over again

Pounded and compounded by Life
yet you remain as you began
far from city lights

unwavering loyalty to country
uncompounded belief
in self and humanity.

---

*Read this and the next poem in tandem.

Dedicated to individuals who work in rural and underserved areas serving community.
Muse: KN, a good human being, surgeon, and novelist. Her latest book, a quasi-memoir—Kavery Nambisan, *A Luxury Called Health A Doctor's Journey Through The Art, The Science And The Trickery Of Medicine* (New Delhi: Speaking Tiger Books, 2021). For a complete list of her published works, see https://en.wikipedia.org/wiki/Kavery_Nambisan.

The Path(s) Taken*

You took a path
stayed on it

I took the same path
strayed from it

You did what I set out to do
to stay the course

I did what I had to do
find another course.

I took another path I thought I should
little knowing that the new path

would lead me
to the path I should.

*Read the previous poem and this in tandem.

Lost And Not Easily Found[†]

You lost your real self, aged five
Here's why

parents aspire to perfection in self
failing, they flail and flog themselves

shredding self-esteem
bleeding security

they project misdirected aspiration on you
their co-created, recently anointed insecurity

encasing your real self
in the virtual cocoon of perfectionism

ensnaring your bubbly personality
in a web of anxiety

*

Schooled in a corrosive curriculum
of letdowns and put-downs—disappointing! not good enough!

you graduate with high distinction
in poor self-confidence and self-esteem

hyper-organized and calm, outside
a hot mess of mixed-up feelings, inside

as we uncouth say—
carpet, wildly, not matching the drapes

achievements entangled with self-worth
seeking external validation in lieu of internal comfort.

†Read this and the next poem in tandem.

Found And Not Easily Lost[†]

You found your 5-year-old self, aged 35
Here's why

by trial and error
more error and terror

along with pills, potions, and
a slew of sessions

you realized that perfection is unrealizable
here, hereafter, ever and forever

for perfection is a bottomless hole in the Sea of Life
perfectionism, the need to touch bottom

*

By trial-and-error practicing Mental Hygiene
written by long gone seafarers of Life

along with pills, potions, and
a slew of sessions

you stepped off the parental boat on to your Life Boat
took complete charge of your own compass, tiller and sails

slipped off the dock lines, shook-out the sails
headed out of safe harbor practicing to be your own skipper

★

As you navigate the outer harbor
to the open waters of the Sea of Your Life

one hand on tiller
the other trimming sail

Life's shoals and hidden channels are better navigated
with the help of a pilot in the form of a mentor, not a tormentor[‡]

facilitating the practice of Mental Hygiene
here, hereafter, ever and forever.

[†]Read the previous poem and this in tandem.

[‡]Quote from the poem entitled "Question For The Ages," in Cariappa Annaiah's compendium of poems, *Echoes of Epictetus & Arrian*, illustrated by Warsha Lath (Mandeville, LA: Inward-Step Publications, 2021), page 158. In the same book, see the poem on a related topic on page 67 entitled, "Parenting riddle – will it be a question or an affirmation?"

Age And Experience

My hearing is wearing
while work which was wearying
is no longer worrying.

False Expectations

Willie buys lilies for Nellie
expects her to agree with him willy-nilly
Silly Willie!

Muse: Conversation with SSM, KB and AK.

A Plea To Paenibacillus*

You and your ilk
curdle milk.
Do me a favor
off-flavor
bad behavior.

---

*Paenibacillus bacteria curdles milk. Reference: Science Daily, "Dairy researchers identify bacterial spoilers in milk," 2012, https://www.sciencedaily.com/releases/2012/07/120720201531.htm.

Debtor For Life

You helped me
when no one else dared or cared

not with money
organs that gave you life

I incurred a debt
I cannot repay, for

unlike a mortgage
there is no gauge

of how much to pay, of what
to whom, and when it ends.

In all else I pay my dues
as they come due

earning my way
to a debt-free existence

but in this instance the debt is in escrow
unpayable as long as life breathes in me.

Dedicated to organ donors, both living and cadaver, who selflessly pay forward the gift of life.

The Impasse

I see troubles hiding behind your troubled eyes
I see worry and procrastination, and not your decision

What alchemic event will convert your indecision?
Nothing cataclysmic I hope

for while fire turns sand to glass
you are not shatter-proof.

You will not admit to your fragility
I am unable to disable your inability . . .

Quandary Of Laundry

Do I
rub it
scrub it
wet it
spin it
dry it
spread it?

Fuck it!
To The Cleaners it is.

The quandary
of not doing your own laundry?

The Cleaners clean
your wallet gets lean.

The Unwrapping

Our friend Michelle
Chocolatier by profession

possessor of many skills—
baker, horticulturist, landscaper, craftswoman, weaver . . .

an artist who heeds the call of Teles
Goddess of Perfection

patience of Job for all things inanimate and animal
we, her friends, are the beneficiaries of her largesse

which comes in many ways
friendship, warmth, thoughtfulness, and

her confections! These days,
we receive fruitcake

a rectangle of delicious brandied goodness
wrapped in layers of plastic film to keep the goodness within

with each layer's start and finish
blending with the layer beneath

keep breathing and be patient, one counsels
as frustration builds at the finger-tips—

Why cannot you be more accessible?
Why so wrapped-up in layers of your own creation?

—trying to unwrap the seemingly unwrap-able
try one must, since therein lies relationship

sensing the goodness under wraps
we engage and unwrap

gently prying away layer by layer
the mask of a reserved personality

reserve built over years
a hedge against fears

fears of adversity, and
the personality of others

over time, with patience and perseverance
marveling at the intricate layering of a complex personality

we uncover in all its naked glory, the fruit of a friend's labor
a paradigm for uncovering fruitful relationships.

Day Dreams

Dark-thirty*
time of night

darkness unbroken
dawn unbroken too

sun asleep
beneath the horizon

finishing its dream
of the day to come.

*Dark-thirty: military slang; early hours before daybreak 3.30 or 4.30 a.m. Reference: Oxford English Dictionary, https://www.oed.com/search/dictionary/?scope=Entries&q=dark+thirty.

Hair-trigger

Extreme anger
begets angor*
begging the question
is the cause worthy of the effect
or is the effect waiting for a cause?

*Angor: Severe anxiety and chest pain thought to be psychosomatic. Reference: Oxford English Dictionary, https://www.oed.com/search/dictionary/?scope=Entries&q=angor.

The Price Of Living

is always worth it
for those who can pay

for me, at times
my life appears unworthy of this world

when in doubt, I look at you my love
and find myself unworthy of you too

when will I learn, my worth is my own
not owned by the world or you?

Controlled Flight Into Terrain (CFIT)*

We see fit
to fit relationships into our lives
rather than our lives into relationships

When that doesn't work
we see fit to retro-fit relationships
losing sight of situational reality

which is when CFIT occurs, as
relationships crash and burn
flying into ground reality.†

*CFIT, pronounced see-fit, acronym for an aviation accident descriptor. Reference: Wikipedia, 2024, https://en.wikipedia.org/wiki/Controlled_flight_into_terrain.
†Ground reality—Indian English term to redundantly emphasize the reality of the moment.

Survivor

You bounded into the darkened room
bright-eyed and bushy-tailed

patient, me
novice optometrist, you

personable and watchful, me
personable and professional, you.

Watching your eyes watching mine
noticed confusion flecked with doubt
I prompted, "all good?"

"Yes," you ventured, and before I dilate
I want to run something by my supervisor

supervisor raises no alarm
confirms your observation

you continue where you left off
confidence in your voice and actions.

You recognized dissonance
alert to your inexperience

called for backup
at the right moment.

All marks of a Survivor
I wish you well.

Wait Not, Want Now

Snuggling up to you
like there was no tomorrow, because
there maybe no tomorrow.

Faces Of A Lie

I'm not a liar
you are a denier
cannot face the truth

I'll fake it
until you can't deny
we aren't going to make it

You are a liar
denier of the truth
I think I am a liar too.

The Papers

The court papers signed and sealed, proclaim we are Apart
no need to wait until *Death Do Us Part*

I pick up the cup of my Life once overflowing with
a hot brew of leaves from our collective lives, now long dry

sluice the amalgamated sludge of a failed relationship
with the clear waters of solo existence, and

uncover golden nuggets of my former self
long lost to the sand and gravel of collective existence.

The Importance Of *And*

To Be
To Have
To Do

That is the question.

To Be, *and*
to Have, *and*
to Do, *and* be a Good Human

This is the answer.

Muse: Travel writer and journalist, Lesley Blanch's lyrically written, genre-setting group biography of a unique set of women. Lesley Blanch, *The Wilder Shores of Love* (London: John Murray, 1954). And, has never been out of print since then! Lesleyblanch.com, 2024, https://lesleyblanch.com/books/biography/the-wilder-shores-of-love/.

Perspective

is not prescription
take it, no price
leave it, no price to pay
in time, it is appraised, praised, and prized.

More Perspective On Perspective

Perspective
is not on loan

perspective
neither opinion nor advice

situationally aware point of view
based on experience, personal or otherwise

take all, none,
"x" of it

you accept any of it, absorb it
becomes yours not mine.

Cross-sectionist—Longitudinalist—*And/Or?*

No sense of History— I don't care
that is history, and His Story mostly

The Here and Now—that I care
my story mostly, not a Mystery

Lived reality is my reality—so there
why should I care about History, someone else's Story?

*

Cross-sectionist, all very well
hear another reality

*

When you line up Cross-sectionists' you get
one long chain

beads on a thread, the thread of Life
we are strung backwards on the common thread

run your fingers over each Cross-sectionist—past
you will read the Braille of History.

*

All very well, Longitudinalist!
hear another reality

∗

History is their lived reality, not mine—my reality
shaped by situational reality, is not theirs

∗

Choose not to tear your page from the Book of History
choose *and* not *or*—we are but bumps of starts and stops
in the Book of Life.

Three C's

Closed spaces, Crowded places, and Close-contact
Three C's
best avoided during pandemics.

Closed, Chattering, and Confused mind, thoughts colliding
Three C's
always best avoided.

Connect with my mind, Come close, and Caress my body
These C's for lovers
never ever avoided!

Sanmitsu*—the three mysteries—
not only Buddha's body, speech and mind
our body, speech and mind too
leave them a mystery at your peril.

*Reference: Tanoshii Japanese, 2023, www.tanoshii-japanese.com/dictionary/entry_details.cfm?entry_id=121123.

Pigeonhole

Classicist!
Modernist!

you try to slot me
not seeing

this pigeon
knows no coop.

Know Thy Enemy—The Elephant In The Room

Pacifist? Filled with righteous anger and contempt
for all things war

Looking for a target to direct your emotions?
You train your sights on the wrong 'X'

neither soldier nor solderer of the bomb circuit
is your enemy

speak not of morality when food, shelter and family are on the line
they work for their daily bread, just as you do, don't you?

your target coordinates are neither
General nor missile manufacturer

they work for power and profit
just as humans do, don't you?

Idealist? In a rush to judgment
you judge unwisely. Redraw the 'X'

your enemies hide in plain sight within all humanity
Politics, Arrogance and Human Frailty.

The Truth About Altruism

Truism, the word, is in altruism
but, is altruism a truism?
or, is altruism even true?

Relationship Want Ad

Looking for friends
with no benefits

to build a relationship
sans relations

desire to relate
not procreate

grace me with your presence
gender, age, race, religion, no bar.

A Time For Everything

A time to count to the cent
a time to time to the second
counting, quantitating everything

not

when I am in your arms and
you in mine

then

we lose count of cents and seconds, and
keep tally—
one kiss, one more, some more, and many more.

Muse: Andamanese, natives of Andaman Islands have only five numbers. Reference: John Lloyd and John Mitchinson, *The Book Of General Ignorance* (New York: Harmony Books, 2006), page 122. A book to unlearn your learning.

Gone Away

Passionate memories like fallen autumn leaves
golden, red, and dry

gathered in a pile by winds of change
outside the door to past Loves

Fear not your past versions, trust your present
open the door, let old flames swirl around you

for a fleeting moment enjoy warm virtuality
as you happily return to reality.

Passionate memories like fallen autumn leaves
golden, red, and dry—go away and return.

Caution! Eavesdropper On-Board

I hate my pregnancy bloat!
    y'all desired progeny
I hate my morning sickness
    you think I like it in here?
I hate my widening hips and lumbar lordosis
    I didn't ask to be born

Oh! My back hurts!
I can't stand to see my wife suffer!

Parents, choose your words as you whine
your child is listening on the party line.

Acknowledge your pain, and recast perspective
else your faux hate may imprint for real in child prospective.

In An Infinite Loop

your love for me
my love for you.

Either—And—Neither

It's the journey say the sages
'tis the goal say the pragmatists

you say, either
I say, and.

Could it be neither, if
you enjoyed the journey, reached the goal

got what you always wanted, and
did not like what you got?

Infinite Prejudice

Humans discriminate
arrayed on the prejudice spectrum.

Tru dat.*

most muddle in the middle and to the left during good times
muddle-less in the middle and to the right when times are bad.

Tru dat.

All humans say, I am not racist and not my ancestors-keeper
we are not holding you back, get over it.

Tru dat.

Here's the rub.
Racist mobs of yesteryear disappeared

into households
heart and minds intact.

What was many became few
few met few and begat few

prejudices intact, few became many. Racism is dead, Long Lives Prejudice!

Sadly, tru dat.

Muse #1: Phil Ochs in the song "Love Me, I'm A Liberal," from his 1960 live album, Phil Ochs In Concert. Reference: Wikipedia, 2024, https://en.wikipedia.org/wiki/Love_Me,_I%27m_a_Liberal.
Muse #2: William Kunstler in the documentary by Emily and Sarah Kunstler, *Disturbing The Universe*. References: Wikipedia, 2024, https://en.wikipedia.org/wiki/William_Kunstler:_Disturbing_the_Universe; BBC.com, 2017, https://www.bbc.com/news/magazine-40124781; The New Yorker, 2010, https://www.newyorker.com/magazine/2010/06/28/life-with-father-2.

*McGraw-Hill's *Dictionary of American Slang and Colloquial Expressions* Copyright © 2006 by The McGraw-Hill Companies, Inc. All rights reserved. Retrieved in 2021, from https://idioms.thefreedictionary.com/Tru+dat.

Halo Family

Some families feud, bleed, and
feed on the bleed, evermore, until

they bleed no more
which is to say, they are dead!

Others feud, bleed, staunch the bleed, and
co-exist ever after

Many feud—bleed—staunch in vain
muscle memory makes them feud again

My family sees red, feuds and draws no blood
our blood stays in its vein lane.

Family And Friends

Family is blood
for most, family is no more than blood

For me, family is blood, and
friends are bloodier.

Least Bad One*

crucial to pick when all choices are bad
say the experts

not easy, all I have is the bulldozer of inexperience
not a pick.

uneasy, when clarity of inexperience is soon clouded
by the experience of nuance

clarity at any given time
rarely clear at any other.

*Andrea Stocco, Chantel S. Prat and Lauren K. Graham, "Individual Differences in Reward-Based Learning Predict Fluid Reasoning Abilities," *Cognitive Science* 45 (2021): e12941, https://doi.org/10.1111/cogs.12941.

Keep It Real

Humor and Hope, grease
the wheels of humanity

in paucity
weighed down by reality

in excess,
slip into unreality.

IBGYBG*

I'll Be Gone, You'll Be Gone
before long

I'll Be Gone, You'll Be Gone
the Universe lives on

make a choice
before long

be woebegone
about going, or

be a better human
before long.

---

*Muse: I'll Be Gone. You'll Be Gone (IBGYBG) was a phrase and acronym used by Wall Street traders referring to the short-termism which was prevalent before the Great Recession of 2007. Reference: Steven Brill, *Tailspin. The people and forces behind America's fifty-year fall—and those fighting to reverse it* (New York: Alfred A. Knopf, 2018). This is a revelatory book that should be widely read but isn't.

Know Thyself!

What?
Never did!

Six Days Later—Was That You?

Back on campus, southern summer afternoon, clear blue sky
Sun leaning west, westerlies fanning my back

peripheral vision, 2 o'clock position, movement above me,
300 feet, solitary bird, wide wingspan, white feathers, black
legs, yellow beak—Great White Egret

flapping ungainly as big birds do on takeoff, gaining altitude,
then, laborious clockwise turn

seeking lift from thermals
circular turn on outstretched wings
occasional flap

wheel—flap—wheel—flap and altitude
like a dance routine, kick—turn—kick—turn and step

I watched, mesmerized by the slow and graceful routine
the wonder of soaring flight
gradually ascending a thermal chimney

moving in ever widening circles away from me
as wind shear leaned the thermal

nearing ceiling altitude, almost a mile away, diminished but
still discernible, sudden banked turn and wings flap with great
gusto in the slipstream of a fast lateral current

rapidly becomes a speck and
one with the aerial haze.

Spell broken, I realize, the thermal was right above your office,
and the bird's compass heading—due East
to your sweet home Alabama!

Reality and learning dictate—coincidence
Imagination and whimsy demur—*Egretta alba* was that you?

This poem is dedicated to the memory of TAP, mentee and colleague, killed in a car accident on August 16th, 2020, six days prior to the bird sighting.

Westerlies—wind originating from the West (winds are named from the direction of origin while water currents by the direction of destination); ceiling altitude—maximum flying height; for herons, including *Egretta alba*, 5000-6000 feet (determined by radar tracks, reference: María Mateos-Rodríguez, and Felix Liechti, "How do diurnal long-distance migrants select flight altitude in relation to wind?" *Behavioral Ecology*, 23, no. 2 (2011): 403-409).

Like A Lump

I am
Part of your life
For life

Loveless

Is love lost
if love was never found?

Is love, lost
if love was never lost, but ground to dust

in the millstones of neglect
driven by the waterwheel of narcissism?

Caveat Emptor!

Teachers and mentors
do not wear
the crown of knowledge.

BC And AD Meet BC And AC*

Eras marked by a remarkable event
complete with dramatis personae
converted, un-converted, and unlikely to be converted!

One wishes reality was not what it is
but it is, so be it
What was then is not now.

---

*Before COVID and After COVID; BCE and CE are preferred abbreviations for BC and AD respectively.

Dear Lover Dear

Conversation is not a string of emoticons
emotions neatly encapsulated in emojis
strung in a conversation thread

No Magi to consult, nor a Magus am I
neither sage nor sorcerer, so
speak to me in sentence strings

give me pearls, not of wisdom, but
how you feel about yourself and me and I will do the same
together we will intertwine ties that bind.

The Ledger

In the ledger of my days
the record of my life, in the past
I readily filled the recrimination column
not the one labelled how to do this better

In the ledger of my days
the record of my life, presently
I readily switch column entries to
recast perspective.

Humorous Note: Don't attempt this in financial accounting!

Where Did I Misplace It?

Keep it in sight
to gain insight.

Ladder Of Life

Rung by rung
climb the ladder of Life

take a firm grip of the rung in front of you
hit your immediate mark and step up

next rung is front and center
next step is clear

At this point in time everything's fine
you're doing fine, stay on the line.

To fall from the ladder of Life
when no one has greased the rungs

focus on the top-most rung
not the one in hand—the matter at hand

you have eyes on the prize, not front and center
do this a few times, miss a step and next step is unclear

At this point in time, it's a matter of time
before you misstep as you overreach, and slide down the line.

Muse: Exhortation used by close friend DB.

This And That Way

Humans were this way
before you were born.

Humans will be that way
long after you die.

The world will change
in many different ways

And, humans will change with change
but not in three important ways

Weakness, Venality and, when they
can get away with it, Viciousness.

Humans were this way
before you were born.

Humans will be that way
long after you die.

Know this as you live

And, don't do unto yourself
what others do to you.

From the grab-bag of human qualities, we possess
identify, greedily grab and make these your own:

Strength to defend
Trustworthiness to stand tall
Kindness to the end, and

Perseverance to nurture them all.

My Drink and I

one, to
loosen my tongue

two, to
lose my inhibition

three, to
souse my thoughts

many drinks a day
keeps myself away

I am my drink.

Muse: "I thought I would drown my sorrows by drinking, and then figured out that my sorrows could swim"—Oscar Ramirez Castaneda's biological father, Tranquilino Castaneda in "Finding Oscar" an episode of *This American Life*, the weekly radio program which aired in May 2012.

The Optimistic Pessimist

Sure, I hop onto your hope
but have no hope that
there is any hope.

No, not being clever
merely pragmatic-realism.

Leave Your Mark

If you tread on the trodden path
does the trodden path tread on you?

Design My Funeral?

Design your funeral before it is too late
urged a funeral home advertisement.

Design my funeral?
I haven't designed my Life!

Witness my funeral, I will not
but, I sure am witness to my Life.

Design my life before it is too late
Wait! Can I design my Life?

Sure, you can, suggest the theologians
Hand over to Higher Authority and watch the design unfold.

By Design, may well be, but
shouldn't I, by design, design My Life?

My Kind Of Optimist

Neither diehard Pangloss
nor cheery Pollyanna
but an optometrist
who slips the right diopter of perspective
into the phoropter* called attitude
to focus on the hot cup of tea in her hands.

*Instrument to measure refractive error used by eye care doctors.

The Eulogy

Oh! I heard your beautiful words
from across the farthest field . . .

. . . a lovely person, such humor, heart of 24K gold, humanitarian,
great father, mother, brother, sister
. . . high praise almost worthy of sainthood

I don't care a fuck what you say now
doesn't affect me. Why?

Because, you dummy, I'm dead and cannot be raised!
Matters little to me what you say and how you say it

You didn't care to give me those roses when I was alive
Don't bother to leave them on my grave.

Muse: "Give me my flowers while I am living" a popular gospel saying made famous by various artists, one of whom was the great soul exponent, Solomon Burke who in a 1983 Washington, D.C. nightclub performance said, "Don't give me my flowers when I'm dead and gone, give me my flowers while I'm living." Reference: "Medley: Monologue (The Women Of Today)/Hold What You've Got/He'll Have To Go," from the album, *Soul Alive* (Cambridge, MA: Rounder Records Corp, 2002).

Pull And Push

Pull and Push, a pain and a problem
for semioticians,* other-icians, and common folk, too.

Pull and Push of daily living come from without and within
and cause emotions to rise and fall like ocean tides do

Fight not like an immovable rock on the beach
for sand will shift where rock once stood

Like sea creatures big and small, lose not your identity
and ride the ebb and flow of Pull and Push.

*Semiotics is the science of signs, symbols and symbolism; the action terms pull and push, resist graphical illustration and represent a unique problem for semioticians, according to Henry Dreyfuss in his landmark and very readable compendium of symbols (Henry Dreyfuss, *Symbol Sourcebook*, an authoritative guide to international graphic symbols (New York: John Wiley & Sons, Inc., 1984) page 30).

The Fever

Heat from within, heat of passion,
ever in heat, every session
body friction, our only friction

our fever, for one another, forever.
That was then,
then, came now

Now, the virus gives us fever, not one another
It took a miasma amongst us
to expose the miasma between us

Muse: Reports of increased domestic violence, worldwide, following stay-at-home orders during the first COVID-19 pandemic.

Perception Of Forgiveness

Pick it up from where I come in
not from the top where you want me to begin

Begin from the beginning
your bloody ancestors are in your blood

Is there any wonder why
the forgiven remain unforgiven?

Consider A Void . . .

some see all black and empty
some see black and full of meaning
some, black and a beautiful sight to behold

others see loss and grief,
others see a gap bridged by the tincture of time
others, a space to live in

I, an outlier, see neither blackness nor emptiness
I see no loss, gap or space
I see fullness and happiness.

On the spectrum of life, we humans cannot avoid
there is no resolution to a void, it remains as is.
Perception on a spectrum determines reality.

Dedicated to all outliers.

Infinite Shade

How many shades of gray?

The spectrum in all humans, things and situations, dictates

As many as you wish.

Gray, the color of nuance.

Lovers

They came through the subway train doors

She, petite, expressive, beautiful eyes only for him
purple nail polished fingers clasped around his neck
making private and all points body contact in a public space.

He, tall, callow youth, trying to act nonchalant, blathering about
schoolwork in a losing battle with his and her raging hormones,
hands over nether region, no doubt hiding a pulsating erection.

I, fellow traveler, male, been there, done that, traveling back in
time, silently wishing their future selves, love after lust, and lust
for communication on all points.

Muse: An anonymous couple on the Metro in Bangalore, India.

Moving On

Our love for one another, a onesie
of halfsies from each other

You opened the snaps
to accommodate, another.

Don't bother, keep your half
I have found another.

My Warmth Returns

You are back, issues unresolved
you are back, is all I care

snuggling, back to front
our priorities, back to front

we slide into unreality
as you slide into me.

Truth be told
physiological need trumps reality.

Warmed by you and the blanket of acceptance
warmth returns to my soul

as we do the wrong thing
for the right reason.

A Question
Or,
My Life, According To Electrons

Launched at birth into panorama and multi-dimensions,
I choose to navigate with 2D blinkers

Adrift in a sea of humanity
I anchor myself to avatars

Flooded by actual reality
I am immersed in virtual reality

Here now, and lost in my digital romance
Is there recompense for the absence of presence?

Muse: Paul Kalanithi, *When Breath Becomes Air* (New York: Random House, 2016).

Authenticity Of Rawness

Raw honey, so yummy
I love my raw Honey

honey, raw and unfiltered, so authentic
like my Honey, raw, and with me, unfiltered.

Muse: M and E.

Inconvenient Lie

Standing in a railway station
I wait, cold in body and soul.

some days, the train approaches, on other days
I await the departed train

alone in this journey
though warmed by family, friends, and familiarity
I carry my baggage, The Truth locked inside

Good days, I finger the keys
bad days, I burnish the lock.

The Truth—acceptance. Necessary,
cathartic for clarity of body and soul,
unpalatable, too bitter to swallow and inconvenient

Inconvenient Lie will do for now, while
I wait to emerge from chrysalis.

But,
will I?

Muse: Elia Kazan's 1957 production of Budd Schulberg's *A Face In The Crowd*, starring Andy Griffith and Patricia Neal, and distributed by Warner Bros.

Frenzied Love

Manipulate—me
tie me in knots

Possess—me
call no exorcist

Shape—me
I'm malleable

Handcuff—me
to your priorities

I offer you myself
all of mine is yours

As I lose myself in yourself
I willingly lose my self and worth.

Address Not Found . . .

. . . said the thought-server in my brain
as it returned my fears, to sender

A reminder that, version 1.0, my fearful self
my mind, no longer, remembers.

Take Heed, No Second Edition

Your Life is an Edition of One.
No one, can edit the one you are
except you.

Self-counsel and seek counsel
to error-correct on the fly
your First and only Edition.

Awake In The Wake Of A Shooting Star

I hitched myself to your rising Star
star-struck by your starlight
too starry-eyed to realize
that traveling in your stardust
I was inhaling cosmic dust
spiraling out of your hot and theoretical persona.

Like a true believer
I sat in the front row
of what I now know, is a public magic show
applauding your brilliance, while
forgiving your proclivity to forget your proclaimed civility and
publicly belittle my intelligence.

You are now past me
intent on a mission to save Heaven
on a trajectory out of my Universe
bedazzling others into submission
while I spiral in slow motion to *terra firma*
bobbing in the solar wind of ancient memories.

Speak Oracle!

Be situationally aware
both feet on the ground and all senses open

Be direct
neither elusive, evasive nor subversive

Honesty in interactions and relationships
is another word for Happiness.

Parting Shot

I love and need you
you make me wet
She makes you wet

Desperate for comfort
my physical needs
against my wishes

seeks you under the comforter
one more time too many.
I cried, tried not to, as I came

Alone, under the comforter
with you still in me, I am left with one thought
Comforter, comfort me, not her.

Waiting For The Spring Flood

We should be happy, but we ain't

We should be together, but we ain't

Our river of happiness, once free flowing

flows in eddies around sunken wrecks of torpedoed trust.

We await a Spring Flood of Hope and Renewal

But will it float our wrecked relationship?

Rising waters do not lift leaky boats.

Muse: The Mississippi River which crests periodically in response to heavy rains or snow melt in the catchment area.

Best Fit

Fit exercise to fitness, not
fitness to exercise

Match expectations to resources, not
resources to expectations.

Muse: MF, colleague, friend, entrepreneur, aspiring Mayor of New Orleans, and fitness maven.

Wolf In Sheep's Clothing

Anamenis* is tricky.

Emesis of facts, it ain't

facts go missing

Therein hides

nemesis of truth

amnesia.

*Anamnesis: A recalling to mind; recollection.
Reference: Webster's Revised Unabridged Dictionary, 1913.

Never Again*

Never Again
rarely, never
commonly, ever

again and again.

Never Again
ever in bed with
Not Able

again and again.

Never Again
an over-promise
humans cannot keep

again and again.

Never Again
too much of a jump from reality to ideal
for weak, venal and vicious humans

again and again.

Never Again
maybe Law of the Land, more or less
but, here's a news flash! Humans are lawless

again and again.

The way from Here Again to Never Again
is no expressway, but a long way
slipping and sliding on the black ice of human frailty

again and again

Never Again can happen, but not in a flash
Over generations of perseverance to the cause
Working locally to make change, and keeping it real

Again and Again.

*Muse: A quote attributed to Amal Clooney, human rights lawyer and keynote speaker, at the 2018 Massachusetts Conference for Women, "There's a long way from #MeToo to never again." Reference: BostonGlobe.com, 2018, https://www.bostonglobe.com/metro/2018/12/06/there-long-way-from-metoo-never-again/VfaLihkmDtHkoCGkvdvGBO/story.html?p1=Article_Recommended_ReadMore_Pos2.

At the Hospital Of No Return

tubes in all my tubes
as I go down the tubes

hooking my fingers
into nooks and crannies

holding onto Life
as Styx flows beneath

Clawing back to normalcy
in a place with no privacy

"Still fighting." "Yes, I am!"*
Everyone else is, for me, so am I!

Life is not a monolith
all glassy and smooth

if I can find nooks and crannies
Why can't You?

*Muse: Family friend, NA. Losing her battle with cancer, in a semi-comatose state, she heard a nurse tell me, "She is still fighting" and forcefully responded, "Yes, I am!" before lapsing into silence.

Did You Feel It?

I came by with a bouquet

in my eyes.

You were away, missed you.

My eyes painted your room

with love and respect.

The Earth, And 10 Things I Got For Free

Parents, two
genetic and epigenetic makeup, four
born with all bits and pieces, eight
mother's milk, nine
microbiome, ten
myself, one

And, relatives, for lagniappe.*

---

*Pronounced lann-yap, a little extra or bonus, Louisiana French via Spanish Creole via Andean Quechua. References: New Oxford American Dictionary; Wikipedia, 2024, https://en.wikipedia.org/wiki/Lagniappe.

Yes, I can count to ten and each number is relevant. Solve the riddle! Solution at the end of the book.

The Olfactory Connection

I smell
as I smell, you.

I hold my nose
you, yours

The smell of humans
living, dying and dead

is no different
for you and I.

Muse: "A combination of grassy notes with a tang of acids and a hint of vanilla over an underlying mustiness, this unmistakable smell is as much a part of the book as its contents," quote from Matija Strlic et al., "Material Degradomics: On the Smell of Old Books," *Analytical Chemistry*, 81, no. 20, (2009), page 8617, American Chemical Society.

Journey's End

Lying next to the other

Lying to one another

Minds once splayed out to the other

Now, tightly shut to one another.

Cord Of Life

Lust calls
sperm enters ovum

Human forms
corded to mother

No cord
no Life

Birth happens
cord detached

sans umbilical cord
Lust calls

Lusty yell
Lust for Life!

Power Of Prayer

God created humans, say the religious
Humans created God, insist the irreligious

No matter

Pray to One, Many or None
if that is what leads to equanimity, and the strength to act

For, act you must.

Anxiety

Did you receive my missive?

I did receive your Valentine

Haven't read it yet

too busy loving you, in my mind

I love you, inhere, in my heart

Do I need to . . . read?

Missing A Match

I want to love you
you want to fuck

I crave a relationship
you crave a fuck

I desire to explore your mind and body
you desire a fuck

It is best,
you go fuck yourself.

Weight Of Comfort

I am unable to reason, and
see no reason to reason
about being unable to reason
when I see comfort food—

To Food! To Food!
Bring me more food!

Alas, one fat dude.

Vapors

High spirits
on spirits
spirits away.

High spirits
sans spirits
rarely goes away.

Young Love

I enter you, as you, me
I know your body, as you, mine

Wondrous, frenzied state of lust
hormones in musth

Tarry! If you can.

Share words and deeds, minds and values, first
Fluids, last.

Sacrificing Your Ease For The Common Good
Or
Not In My Backyard

I won't do it
You won't too.

We won't do it
They won't too.

Who will do it?

So easy to sigh,
and say, so be it . . .

We people
better DO IT!

We Can Have It All

Of course, not!

Where are you?
In some navel-gazing dream?

So full of hubris
expecting to have everything?

If you do have something
that "thing" came about
not only from your endeavors
but also, from the cumulative work
of your indentured slaves—ahem,
your parents
and, a village of other supporters.

You get the idea, don't you?
We cannot have it all.

Hot Cup Of Tea

warms body and soul.

I hold it on days
the sun doesn't shine, and

when my life dwells in the place
the sun doesn't shine, and

when the sun shines
where I want it to shine, and

when the sun shines.

Metaphoric Hot Cup Of Tea

Recall
Recognize
Celebrate

Life's small victories

Clasp
Sip
Savor

Keep the bar low, and see it rise high.

Time Flies

I walk, solo, on a journey
trip unsolicited, unwelcome and uncharted
began while you turned cold on a gurney

Through the plains of my mind, scoured by winds of change
like tumbleweed, I roll, and stop, and roll into oases of memories
to roll on, yet again, to points I know not, where

Time flies, another year passes.
I climb the high desert mesa
to commune with you at sunrise, a sunrise we loved

Like tumbleweed, I roll, and stop, and roll past oases of memories
driven by the breath of life, I speed forward, to points unknown
like tumbleweed, I am losing twigs—of our memories

Time flies, I have you on my mind
I . . . you . . . my . . . mind
I . . . you

I.

Dedicated to all who have lost a partner.

Death Of A Teacher

Standing on the beach of Life, I watch
the treacherous surf of the Great Leveler
claim my teacher, a healer.

Medical school graduating class,
year of my birth.

Pounding surf, levels the beach
and sends emissaries—harbingers of our fate
towards me.

Fellow beach goers, my peers
we walk on warm sand, for now.

The surf, surfs across the beach
as we come ever closer
to the Great Leveler.

The Case Against Insensate Intelligence

Autonomous agents
the living kind
encased wetware
between two ears

exhibit imagination and creativity
alchemy of chemicals, electricity, knowledge
we know all about, and
magic we know little about

imagination and creativity
to do good
and
evil.

Autonomous agents
the non-living kind
encased hardware
running software

exhibit generative artificial intelligence
alchemy of electrons in motion
statistics in action, and
a black box we know little about

Networking ability
to do good
and
evil

Humans, in our rush to do good and evil
replace at our own peril
irregular rhythms of humanity with
persuasive algorithms of inhumanity.

Shredding Paper, Only

I shred, you shred, we shred.
Wish we would shred
stuff that shreds our lives.

Matrimonial Bliss

Woman seeks man

man seeks woman

man seeks man

woman seeks woman

they seek them.

Be that as it may.

For Happiness Ever After

human seeks human.

Summery Sunday Siesta

Southern breeze, flows North
warm and comforting

Languorous and libidinous
in equal parts

A pleasant state of mind
as Northern blood, flows South.

Muse: Robin Williams in "Robin Williams Live on Broadway (2002)" one of his HBO stand-up specials. Reference: Wikiquote, 2024, https://en.wikiquote.org/wiki/Robin_Williams.

The Truth Comes Bedraggled

You don't have a pedigree?
I don't listen to the degreeless

You don't have power?
I listen less to the powerless

You don't have wealth?
Talk to me when you have some, and keep moving

No station in life that I deem worthy?
My listening train does not stop for the unworthy

Self-confined in ivory towers of ilk
drunk on the power of my degrees

clothed in the arrogance of privilege
blinded by the brilliance of hubris

I welcome truth only when
truth comes decked in the puffery of

pedigree, power, and privilege.

Dead-End

How can I increase my accessibility
to your inaccessibilities
when you slam shut the doors
to your accessibilities?

Weaver Of The Historical Record

history of strife

Us versus Them
His story and Hers

is a multi-braided tale

History is not equifinal*
neither equal nor final

unless all voices are heard.

*Equifinal: having the same end or result.
Reference: New Oxford American Dictionary.

8-22-8

The dimensions of my spindle in years
the spindle of work experience
in the loom of life
this is done, replaced by a new one.

The dimensions of my spindle in years
the spindle of life experience
in the loom of life
undone and yet spinning.

Aspire

Walk this Earth
make the choice
with a grrr . . . or
with *envergure**
with caliber.

**Envergure* is the French word for wingspan. When used metaphorically to describe a person, it suggests caliber. Reference: Anonymous, *The Persecution of My Father*, American Experience, Article, PBS.org, 2019, https://www.pbs.org/wgbh/americanexperience/features/mccarthy-persecution-my-father/. A poignant account of the author's childhood in 1950s Paris.

My Gifts . . .

of time and things
like perspective
once accepted
is yours, like it was never mine

no retrospective
in my mind
of gifts to you
no mother lode of lists to mine.

Leave No Trace

As we traverse the Universe of Existence
we blaze no trail for others to follow

like contrails that streak the sky
dispersed at the whim of elements

the trail we leave constructed of the ephemera of existence
—genes, station, talent, luck, and chance—

marked by toil and tribulations
is a maze to follow.

We Are Links In The Chain Of Continuity

No, not genetic, so passé
The Earth is frenetic with teeming billions

No, not those links.
We are links in the chain of continuity

of apprenticeship, mentorship, wisdom
and what it means to be a human in humanity

We are links in the chain of continuity
of history past—present—future

Adulate not the strong link, Fear not the weak link
We are all weaklings prone to hubris and failure
gone in a geological blink

We are links in the chain of continuity
a multi-threaded linkage to life, animate and inanimate

Forge your link the best you can, worry not about conformity
and feel the tug of continuity.

Muse: Bessie Stanley's Famous Poem which appeared in the Lincoln Sentinel, Nov. 30, 1905. Reference: KSGen Web Project, 2024, https://ksgenweb.org/KSLincoln/firstfamilies/stanleybessie.htm.

Means To An End—An Aviation Metaphor

People with ignoble and noble goals
at the start
have the same start
cannot be set apart

piloting similar craft
selfsame takeoff attitude
flight path, and
cruising altitude.

Their compass bearing and
where they land is where
the ignoble and the noble
are set apart

one,
does the right things for the wrong reasons
the other,
does the right things for the right reasons.

Tyranny Of Longevity[†]

99 And Counting

At 99, age is more than a number
all bets are off
bookies have left the building.

*

Spoilt

Blessed by the fortune of no misfortune
I expected to go on forever
untouched by the hand of ill-luck and bad health

sadly, inevitably
entropy inbuilt in all things
disordered my life

touched by the hand of ill-luck and bad health
unhappy about all and everything
happy about none and nothing

I am now all alone
grieving my inability to be able
with no reserve for recovery

independent for eons
I find myself
dependent upon others not of my choosing

Absent self-reflection, independence
the freedom from dependence brings with it spoilt behavior,
snap judgment, and inability to accept the help of strangers.

★

Prayer For Freedom

The strength of freedom for 99 years
now working against me
I will overcome

The fortitude that kept me independent at 99
will return
to cast off the yoke of freedom

I will accept the unacceptable, unpalatable, and the
ultimate tyranny of unexpected longevity
to live in redefined dignity, 99 years and counting.

†Read the poems on pages 280-283 in tandem.

Now, Not Later*

Who you are
when you are
infirm

is times two
who you are before you are
infirm.

Pre-morbid state of mind, body, and soul
harbinger of misery or relative equanimity
of our inevitable morbid fate.

Who you are
before you are
infirm

is not pre-ordained by Nature, Nurture, Heaven, or Earth
don't hold forth that all is set in stone
stone is what will hold you down.

Pay heed to your pre-morbid state
before you are infirm
else, you will curse Nature, Nurture, Heaven, and Earth.

*Read the poems on pages 280-283 in tandem.

Does It Matter?*

Is this love, or
is this pressure
driven by the oceanic momentum of
filial duty, fealty to family, fear of deity

Does it matter?

It doesn't.
I am in the here and now
caretaker, caregiver, care-everything
cemented to the cause

Does it matter?

It does.
Bad days, cement feels like the deadweight it is
other days I see self-chosen shackles with a key in the lock
Bad days, I unlock mind and soul, not always the body

Good days, I unlock, escape,
on the run, message
—bye, left home—
for now.

*Read the poems on pages 280-283 in tandem.

Lower Latitude Lover

I'm a lower lover
love all things south

southern skies, constellations, elements,
food, fun, and people

north is a tease
south is where the action is

the north
stimulates and arouses

the south
entrance to good, bad, sublime, ecstasy, and evil

gateway to humanity
is where it's at.

I sink to my knees, entranced
as I inhale your warm and unique fragrance.

Hair Of The Goat

In India, nothing is wasted
not even hair of the goat
goes a saying

South Indian by birth
North American Southerner by choice
I rejoice the mix of culture and mirth that informs my work

Muses strike me from nook and cranny
common threads in the uncommon and disparate
where others see none

More than nine Muses inform my poetry
none forsaken, all taken
even hair of the goat.

Letting Go, Not Goodbye

You are departing
for parts known and unknown

I know where you are going
a place you want to go

I know not where you are headed
for that is for you to explore

grow and blossom
in ways only you can and should.

As you release the slip ropes
mooring your Life Boat to our relationship dock

I fumble with a tangled jumble of metaphorical ropes
binding our boats in a raft

but untangle I will
safe in the knowledge

that our boats possess
a communicator within easy reach.

Solution for poem on page 250

Parents are 2 in number; each parent contributes one of two parts of their genetic and epigenetic makeup, 1 + 1 + 1 + 1 = 4; all bits and pieces are those that can be seen on the body; collectively, they add up to eight: eyes, ears, nose, mouth, hands, feet, genitalia and anus; mother's milk contains 9 essential amino acids; and, in 2017 the human skin microbiome had 10 bacterial classes. Lines 1, 2, and 6 represent individual entities which add up to 7 (2 + 4 + 1); lines 3, 4, and 5 name collective entities which can be represented by the numeral 1, thus line 3 is 7 + 1 = 8, line 4, 8 + 1 = 9 and line 5 is 9 + 1 = 10.

Acknowledgements

Jennifer Dubin, my editor, your steady guidance makes my work stronger. Is the Pope Catholic?! Thank you.

Thanks to a small circle of friends and family, who over the years are a great sounding board: Shoba Srinatha, Jennifer Dubin, S. S. Meera, Kiran Bettadapur, Daphne Bell, Warsha and Goutam Lath, Uthika Singh Mankothia, Marissa Fahlberg and Eric Williams, Amanda and Giorgio Zenere, Aparajita Lath, Sarah Chatta, Jovita Crasta, Ilka Arun Netravali, Nell Bond, Carol E. Morse, Bobby Cherayil, Thomas P. Gillis, Martin Heyder, Pawan Bhushan, Ramnik Xavier, Blake Schouest, Kristin Merino, Claiborne M. Christian, Carolina Allers Hernandez, Michelle N. Sullivan-Bernard, Robert Blair, and Michelle Connole. And, more recently, Kavery Nambisan.

Amitinder Kaur, wife, and friend, who is my coarse and fine filter, always, thank you.

Subject Index

2 not 1, 19

Ability, 2, 69, 115, 266
Able, 2, 159, 246, 280
Absent, 122, 160, 280
AC, 213
Accessible, 174, 272
Accounting, 19, 215
Achievement, 164
Acknowledgement, 122, 197, 261
Action, 2, 6, 59, 114, 180, 254, 266, 284
Active, 153
AD, 213
Address, 238
Adjective, 36
Adult, 7, 12, 13, 120
Advice, 187
Age, 4, 76, 80, 139, 147, 158, 164, 166, 168, 194, 280
Aggression, 68
Aid, 61n
AK, 169n
AL, 92n
Alabama, 208
alba, *Egretta*, 208
Alchemy, 172, 266
Alcohol, 68, 90, 220, 258
Alexander The Great, 5n

Alexandria, 71
Algorithm, 106, 266
Alone, 4, 18, 119, 152, 236, 242, 280
Alternate reality, 50
Altitude, 208, 279
Alto, 30
Altruism, 12, 193
American, 285
Amnesia, 46, 245
Analgesia, 46
Anamnesis, 245
Ancestor, 104, 200, 228
Anchor, 107, 110, 234
And, 185
Andamanese, 195n
Anger, 102, 177, 192
Angor, 177
Answer, 72, 108, 139, 148, 185
Anticipation, 94
Antidote, 20
Anxiety, 13, 94, 164, 177, 255
Appearance, 33
Appraisal, 186
Archivist, 71
Arms, 8, 30, 106, 110, 146, 195
Arrival, 47
Arrogance, 192, 271
Arsonist, 71

Art, 70, 105, 174
Artificial intelligence, 266
Artnik, Alenka, 160n
Aspire, 60, 164, 275
Assistant, 155
Astrologer, 148
Attitude, 151, 224, 279
Au Naturel, 31
Authentic, 235
Author, Anonymous, 275n
Authority, 138, 223
Autonomous, 266
Autumn, 196
Avatar, 76, 158, 234
Avaya, 76
Aviation, 179n, 279
Awesome, 52

Backed Up, 136
Bacteria, 81n, 170, 287
Bad, 170, 200, 204, 236, 280, 283, 284
Baggage, 101, 236
Bagh, 44
Bangalore, 231n
Barcha, Mercedes, 27n
Barricade, 54
BC, 213
BCE, 213n
Beach, 112, 114, 226, 265

Behavior, 12, 170, 280
Belief, 89, 139, 162, 240, 254
Belong, 23
Beloved, 6, 76
bi-Coastal, 84
Billiard, 62
Binary, 12, 36
Bipolar, 36
Bird, 72, 208
Birth, 218, 234, 253, 265, 285
Bitter, 66, 114, 236
Black, 67, 208, 229, 246, 266
Blame, 8, 13, 67, 153
Blanch, Lesley, 185n
Bloat, 39
Block, 1, 44
Blood, 13, 35, 36, 39, 202, 203, 228, 270
Bloom, 31, 91
Boat, 4, 11, 42, 107, 166, 243, 286
Body, 11, 44, 65, 68, 79, 106, 118, 141, 190, 227, 231, 236, 256, 259, 262, 282, 283, 287
Bomb, 67, 192
Bond, 214
Book, 9, 49, 188
Bookie, 27

Boss, 140
Bra, 112
Braille, 32, 188
Brain, 110, 238
Breakup, 156
Breast-feeding, 16
Breasts, 112
Breath, 10, 38, 171, 174, 264
Brill, Steven, 206n
Brimstone, 59
Broigus, 57
Brother, 67, 68, 225
Bubble, 36
Bucket, Hyacinth, 33n
Buddha, 190
Burden, 111
Burglar, 143
Burke, Solomon, 225n
Buyer's remorse, 83

Caliber, 275
Cancer, 62, 92n, 157, 248n
Cannoli, 78
Car, 61, 132, 209n
Career, 148, 163
Caregiver, 283
Caretaker, 283
Carpet not matching the drapes, 164
Castaneda, Tranquilino, 220n

Caveat emptor, 212
CE, 213n
Challenge, 18, 54
Chance, 10, 56, 62, 68, 105, 147, 148, 277
Change, 19, 62, 89, 112, 142, 154, 196, 218, 246, 264
Chaos, 31, 140
Chapman, Colin, 132n
Charcoal, 32
Charm, 121
Chatta, Harbinder Kaur, 43n
Chatter, 122, 190
Children, 13, 14, 16, 76, 138, 154, 197
China Syndrome, 129n
Choice, 15, 71, 83, 139, 163, 204, 206, 275, 283, 285
Chopel, Gendun, 84n
Chore, 131
Chrysalis, 236
Circus, 11, 14
Civic sense, 206, 260
Clarity, 114, 204, 236
Clarke, Roy, 33n
Classicist, 191
Cleaners, 173
Cleavage, 155n
Clooney, Amal, 247n
Coach, 138

Subject Index 293

Cocktails, 90
Coffee, 58, 105
Cognoscenti, 161
Cohabitation, 137
Cohen, Leonard, 55n
Coincidence, 208
Cold, 37, 146, 236, 264
Color, 31, 65, 116, 230
Comfort, 164, 242, 257, 270
Common good, 260
Common thread, 188, 285
Communication, 72, 231, 241, 271, 272, 286
Compartmentalization, 136
Compass, 166, 208, 279
Competent, 7
Completion, 2
Complicate, 132
Computer, 266
Concept, 132
Confidence, 35, 140, 164, 180
Conflate, 60, 153
Conflict, 5, 8, 13
Conform, 159
Confounder Hell, 124
Confusion, 180, 190

Connection, 251
Conscience, 59
Conscious, 71, 144
Consequence, 59, 129
Constantinople, 71
Consultant, 112
Consume, 12
Contact, 67, 190, 231
Continent, 146
Continuity, 278
Contrails, 277
Contralto, 30
Control, 7, 54, 82, 103, 117, 143, 150, 179
Convenience, 2
Conversation, 214
Convert, 172, 213
Cooking, 49
Coop, 191
Copayment, 138
Correct, 239
Counsel, 155, 174, 239
Count, 19, 91, 158, 195, 280
Couple, 50, 232
COVID, 213, 227n
Crap, 136
Crawfish, 150
Crisis, 28
Critical, 2
Crossroad, 17
Cross-sectionist, 188
Cross-ventilate, 80

Crowd, 150, 190
Crown, 212
Cuddley-duddle, 16
Cuss, 5
Cycle, 38

Dadi, 44
Daymare, 112
DB, 217n
DDR, 121n
Death, 37, 42, 62, 67, 68, 94, 109, 145, 157, 202, 206, 208, 218, 223, 225, 229, 248, 251, 264, 265
Death do us part, 184
Debt, 171
Decision, 172
Default state, 218
Degree, 271
Deity, 283
Deliverable, 60, 159
Delusions, 56
Dementia, 11
Denial, 13, 27
Departure, 42, 47, 286
Dependent, 280
Depression, 13, 134
Desert, 36, 264
Design, 223
Desire, 40, 143, 194, 197, 242, 256
Destiny, 24

Devil, 153
Dice, 10
Dictionary, 121
Difference, 251
Digestion, 116
Digital, 234
Dignity, 281
Dilemma, 7
Diopter, 224
Direct, 192, 241
Disabled, 2
Discover, 109
Discrimination, 93
Discussion, 5
Disorder, 31, 280
Dispute, 5
Diss, 5
Distinction, 164, 279
Distrust, 251, 252
Divorce, 184
Doctor, 94, 158, 162, 265
Dog and bark, 7
Double-Speak, 50
Dramatis personae, 213
Drawing, 32
Dream, 37, 67, 68, 112, 126, 143, 176, 261
Dreyfuss, Henry, 226n
Drill Sergeant, 92
Drink, 220, 258

Drugs, 68
Duality, 87
Dummy, 225
Dust, 2, 80, 211, 240
Duty, 283
Dystopia, 67, 68

E, 235n
Ears, 30, 143, 266
Earth, 39, 54, 250, 275, 278, 282
East, 208
Eavesdropper, 197
Ecstasy, 284
Edition, 239
Education, 54, 271
Efficiency, 2
Egret, Great White, 208
Either, 23, 199
Electrons, 234, 266
Elephant in the room, 71, 192
Elusive, 241
Embrace, 37, 65
Emesis, 245
Emoticons, 214
Emotion, 36, 68, 129, 143, 153, 177, 192, 214, 226
Empathy, 85
Employment, 93, 140
Empty, 42, 47, 55, 229

Emulate, 277
End, 5, 12, 97, 135, 147, 171, 218, 252, 272, 279
Enemy, 48, 192
Energy, 153
Enlightenment, 54
Enough, 18, 66, 102, 154
Entropy, 31, 280
envergure, 275
Epigenetic, 250
Equal, 18, 47, 77, 118, 251, 270, 273
Equanimity, 24, 254, 282
Equifinal, 273
Era, 213
Error, 19, 166, 239
Escape, 68, 283
Essence, 47, 162
Ethnicity, 8
Eulogy, 225
Evanescent, 21
Evasive, 241
Evil, 266, 284
Excellent, 52
Exception, 112
Excoriator, 35
Exercise, 244
Existence, 101, 171, 184, 277
Exorcist, 237

Expectation, 26, 40, 169, 244
Expected, 20, 280
Experience, 71, 80, 101, 168, 180, 187, 204, 274
Expert, 112, 204
Explore, 148, 256, 286
External, 54, 164
Eyes, 30, 38, 68, 126, 129, 155, 172, 180, 217, 231, 249

Facade, 33
Face Value, 9
Fact, 32, 245
Faith, 13, 111
Fake, 183
Family, 22, 38, 48, 139, 192, 202, 203, 236, 283
Fantasy, 21, 103, 130
Farm, 60
Farthest field, 225
Fat, 257
Fat head, 75
Fate, 19, 24, 265, 282
Father, 225
Fear, 174, 196, 238, 278, 283
Fearless, 27
Feet, 23, 112, 241
Female, 110

Feud, 202, 228
Fever, 227
Fiction, 32
Fight, 104, 105, 202, 226, 248
Firefly, 37
Firewater, 68
First impression, 9
First principles, 124
Fit, 179, 244
Fitzgerald, F. Scott, 24n
Flail, 24, 164
Flight, 179, 208, 279
Flood, 61, 234, 243
Flow, 16, 36, 39, 184, 226, 243, 248, 270
Flowers, 225, 249
Fluids, 259
Flying, 179, 208
Focus, 12, 76, 108, 116, 124, 217, 224
Follow, 55, 126, 240, 277
Food, 48, 78, 125, 192, 257, 284
Force-multiplier, 8
Foreknowledge, 148
Forever, 32, 88, 126, 166, 227, 280
Forgiven, 228
Fortitude, 280

Found, 162, 164, 166, 211, 232, 238
Fragile, 172
Free, 79, 171, 243, 250
Freedom, 64, 129, 280
Freezer, 37
Frenzy, 237
Friction, 227
Friend, 48, 87, 101, 107, 122, 125, 174, 194, 203, 236
Frozen, 6, 36
Fruitcake, 174
Fuck, 256
Fuck (as expletive), 92, 143, 173, 225
Funeral, 223
Future, 24, 58, 106, 114, 142, 148, 182, 231, 278

Gambling, 27
Gander, 135
García Márquez, Gabriel, 27n
Garcia, Rodrigo, 27n
Garg, Anu, 56n
Gas, 128
Gender, 93, 135, 194, 269
Generalist, 108
Generation, 2, 104, 247, 228

Generative, 266
Genetic, 250, 278
German, 111n
Gift, 276
Giving, 12
Goal, 199, 279
Goat, 285
God, 111, 223, 254
Goddess, 106, 174
Good, 266, 284
Goodbye, 42, 286
Goose, 135
Gordian Knot, 5
Graham, Sheilah, 24n
Grandeur, 56
Grandmother, 44, 76
Grate, 59
Gratitude, 64, 140, 262, 263
Grave, 225
Gray, 230
Grief, 229
Grip, 23, 103, 217
Ground reality, 179
Guarantee, 35
Guess, 57, 128
Guilt, 59, 68, 145
Gynecoid pelvis, 106

Habit, 122, 144
Hair, 76, 285
Halfsies, 232
Hall of Mirrors, 28

Handcuff, 237
Hands, 23, 49, 99, 102, 224, 231
Happiness, 229, 241, 243, 269
Hardware, 266
Hate, 36, 197
Have-nots, 99
Haves, 99
Head, 62, 75, 92
Healing, 66
Health, 62, 64, 66, 280
Hearing, 102, 168
Hearse, 44
Heart, 36, 70, 71, 116, 200, 225, 255
Heat, 37, 227
Heaven, 240, 282
Hellfire, 59
Help, 5, 61, 71, 100, 111, 167, 171, 261, 280
Hero worship, 240
Heron, 208
Hide, 33, 141, 192, 245
Highballs, 90
History, 150, 188, 228, 273, 278
Holmes, Oliver Wendell, 158
Holy Grail, 2

Home, 38, 118, 208, 223, 283
Homily, 22
Honesty, 69, 141, 241
Honey, 235
Hooton, Gordon, 132n
Hope, 16, 38, 50, 87, 112, 145, 172, 205, 221, 243
Hormones, 37, 39, 112, 231, 259
Hospital, 248
Hot, 6, 37, 164, 184, 240
Hot cup of tea, 71, 224, 262, 263
House, 38, 42, 44, 47, 148, 200
Hubris, 261, 271, 278
Hug, 42, 96
Human, 5, 8, 9, 12, 15, 104, 105, 115, 118, 128, 132, 144, 159, 185, 192, 200, 206, 218, 229, 230, 246, 251, 253, 254, 266, 269, 278
Human frailty, 192, 246
Humanitarian, 225
Humanity, 13, 54, 87, 110, 162, 192, 200, 205, 234, 266, 278, 284

Humankind, 8, 99
Humor, 205
Hunt, 11
Hurricane, 14
Husband, 50

id, 94
Ideal, 60, 192, 246
Identity, 28, 33, 207, 226, 282
Idiot savant, 108
Ignoble, 279
Image, 28, 116
Imagination, 208
Impasse, 172
Impatience, 2, 14
in silico, 106
Inability, 92, 159, 172, 257, 280
Inaccessible, 272
Inanimate, 132, 174, 278
Incognito, 161
Incoming, 54
Independence, 280
India, 45n, 231n, 285
Indifference, 260
Indigent, 145
Individualism, 261
Indulgence, 78
Inexperience, 204
Infants, 12, 16
Inferior, 52

Infidelity, 50
Infinite, 57, 198, 200, 230
Infirm, 282
Influence, 54
Inheritance, 104
Inhibition, 220
Inhumanity, 266
Initiative, 148, 260
Innovation, 26
Insecurity, 18, 122, 164, 255
Insensate, 266
Insight, 116, 216
Insouciance, 34
Inspire, 60
Instinct, 155
Intelligence, 240, 266
Intense, 34
Intern, 98
Intestine, 34
Intrinsic, 117, 258
Intuition, 148
Iraq War, 67n
Island, 101, 114, 146
Isolation, 29

Jaded, 109
James, William, 158n
JD, 4n
Jealousy, 8
Job, 161
JoC, 75n

Jolly the Clown, 11
Journey, 126, 199, 236, 252, 264
Judgment, 19, 192, 280

Kalanithi, Paul, 234n
Kazan, Elia, 236n
KB, 169n
Key, 42, 236, 283
KH, 63n
Killer, 58
Kindness, 16, 64, 218
Kiss, 58, 91, 102, 195
Knife, 13
Knot, 5, 23, 237
Knowledge, 80, 99, 117, 120, 129, 148, 212, 266, 286
Koslow, Sally, 24n
Kunstler, William, 201n

Labor, 2, 118, 174, 261
Ladder, 217
Lagniappe, 250
Lath, Warsha, 167n
Latitude, 150, 151, 284
Laughter, 48
Laundry, 173
Law, 129, 246
Law of unintended consequences, 129

Laying of the hands, 23
Leak, 243
Least bad one, 204
Ledger, 215
Letter, 255
Libido, 112
Library, 71
Lie, 50, 106, 126, 144, 183, 236, 252
Life, 2, 4, 17, 18, 23, 24, 32, 36, 38, 42, 44, 48, 58, 62, 64, 67, 68, 71, 74, 86, 89, 98, 100, 101, 110, 145, 147, 157, 160, 162, 163, 164, 166, 171, 178, 179, 184, 188, 208, 210, 215, 217, 223, 229, 234, 239, 248, 253, 262, 263, 264, 265, 271, 274, 277, 278, 280
Life Boat, 4, 42, 107, 166, 286
Life events, 17
Light, 65, 141, 162
Lightness, 132
Linchpin, 5
Link, 278
Lion, 11
Liquor, 90

Lives, 10, 12, 14, 48, 79, 120, 179, 184, 268
Living, 36, 44, 50, 62, 68, 80, 113, 178, 226, 266
Lloyd, John, 195n
Lock, 28, 42, 236, 283
Logic, 14
Longevity, 280
Longitudinalist, 188
Loom, 274
Loop, 57, 198
Loss, 68, 140, 145, 160, 229, 264
Lost, 80, 92n, 106, 162, 164, 166, 184, 211, 234, 264n
Louisiana, 92n, 150, 151, 250n
Love, 6, 10, 11, 27, 30, 31, 36, 37, 42, 50, 51, 58, 64, 65, 74, 84, 88, 91, 96, 102, 106, 118, 122, 124, 126, 131, 141, 143, 156, 162, 178, 195, 196, 198, 211, 231, 232, 235, 237, 242, 249, 255, 256, 259, 264, 283
Love child, 14
Loveless, 126, 211

Lover, 6, 51, 58, 72, 74, 88, 101, 116, 118, 131, 190, 196, 214, 231, 284
Low hanging fruit, 19
Luck, 10, 62, 135, 277, 280
Lump, 210
Luscomb, Florence, 56n
Lust, 118, 231, 253, 259
Lyme Disease, 80n

M, 235n
Ma, 49
Magi, 214
Magic, 266, 240
Magical thinking, 1
Magus, 214
Mailbox, 72
Main street, 33
Major-domo, 21
Male, 231
Man, 39, 50, 269
Manipulate, 237
Mark, 91, 180, 213, 217, 222, 277
Marriage, 50, 108, 126, 137, 139, 184, 269
Match, 164, 244, 256

Mateos-Rodríguez, M, 209n
Matrimony, 37, 50, 72
Matsuura, Motoo, 140n
Maze, 277
Meditation, 153
Memo, 19
Memory, 30, 32, 42, 46, 49, 68, 71, 76, 143, 196, 202, 240, 263, 264
Ménage à trois, 31
Menagerie, 21
Mendacious, 144
Mental health, 13
Mental Hygiene, 166
Mentee, 86
Mentor, 86, 166, 212, 239, 278
Metaphor, 90, 263, 279, 286
Metro, 231n
Metronome, 120
Mezzo-soprano, 30
MF, 244n
Miasma, 227
Michelle, 174
Microbiome, 250
Micromanager, 7
Military, 176n
Milk, 16, 170, 250
Millstone, 211
Mind, 11, 13, 28, 32, 36, 44, 71, 79, 80, 92, 101, 106, 116, 126, 129, 130, 131, 141, 143, 153, 190, 200, 238, 252, 255, 256, 259, 264, 270, 276, 282, 283
Mine, 67, 276
Misery, 55, 136, 282
Mismatch, 256
Misplace, 216
Missionary, 90
Mississippi River, 243n
Mitchinson, John, 195n
Mob, 200
Model, 277
Modernist, 191
Money, 104, 171
Moon, 72
Mooring, 14, 286
Morality, 192
Morning, 48, 65, 76
Mortgage, 171
Mother, 16, 49, 225, 250, 253, 276
Mother lode, 276
Motivator, 92
Move, 146, 154
Movement, 12, 208
MP, 81n
Multi-dimensions, 234

Subject Index   303

Multiple, 19, 28, 158
Multitasking, 2
Muses, 285
Musth, 259
Mystery, 33, 188, 190

NA, 248n
Nambisan, Kavery, 162n
Narcissism, 28, 211
Nature, 31, 120, 282
Navel-gazing, 60, 261
Neglect, 71, 211
Nellie, 169
Nemesis, 245
Nepotism, 22
Network, 266
Never again, 246
Nightmare, 14
Noah's Ark, 4
Noble, 97, 279
Noblesse Oblige, 97
Non-living, 266
Nook and cranny, 71, 248, 285
North, 84, 270, 284
Nose, 251
Nostalgia, 46
Not able, 246
Not in my backyard, 260
Nuance, 9, 204, 230
Nubile, 155n

Number, 62, 148, 280
Nurse, 16
Nurture, 2, 219, 282

Objectivity, 71
Obligation, 97
Oblivion, 42
Ocean, 114, 226, 265
Ochs, Phil, 201n
Olfactory, 251
Once, 9, 38, 50, 88, 133, 137, 184, 226, 243, 252, 276
Onesie, 232
Opinion, 187
Opportunity, 77, 103, 115
Oppression, 13, 134
Optimist, 102, 221, 224
Optometrist, 180, 224
Oracle, 241
Order, 31
Ordinary, 52
Organization, 116, 164
Organs, 116, 171
Orgasm, 84, 130
Orgy, 31
Origin, 105, 114
Ouija board, 49
Outlier, 229
Ovation, 26
Over-promise, 246

Overreach, 217
Ovum, 253

Pacifist, 192
Paenibacillus, 170
Paige, Satchel, 147
Pain, 68, 94, 126, 197, 226
Pandemic, 190, 213, 227
Pangloss, 224
Panorama, 234
Paper, 48, 184, 268
Parabiosis, 96
Paranoia, 20
Parents, 13, 23, 38, 76, 126, 138, 154, 164, 166, 197, 250, 261
Parity, 57
Parting, 242
Partner, 16n, 60, 109n, 118, 122, 264n
Pas de deux, 31
Passion, 6, 58, 196, 227
Passive, 153
Past, 38, 68, 107, 114, 142, 147, 188, 196, 200, 213, 215, 278
Paternal, 22
Path, 62. 148, 163, 222, 279

Patience, 2, 9, 60, 98. 174
Patient, 98, 180
Patriot, 162
Patronize, 118, 145
Pavlovian, 26
Peace, 18, 39
Pedigree, 271
Pendulum, 147
People, 9, 50, 145, 260, 279, 284
Perception, 107, 117, 228, 229
Perfection, 7, 164, 166, 174
Period, 39
Perseverance, 60, 174, 218, 246
Persistence, 60, 210
Personalities, 19, 158
Personality, 164, 174
Perspective, 25, 114, 120, 186, 187, 197, 215, 216, 224, 276
Pessimist, 221
Peter, 155
Philanthropy, 12
Phone booth, 79
Phoropter, 224
Physiology, 233
Pigeonhole, 191
Pigment, 105
Pitre, Michael, 67n

Plan, 20
Plant, 23, 143
Plants, 31, 91
Polar, 36
Policy, 13
Politicians, 13
Politics, 192
Pollyanna, 224
Poor, 2, 145, 271
Porchio, Antonio, 160n
Possess, 74, 237
Posterity, 38
Potion, 6, 166
Power, 130, 145, 192, 254, 271
Practice, 144, 167
Pragmatist, 199, 221
Praise, 186, 225
Prayer, 254, 281
Pregnancy, 197
Prejudice, 200
Pre-morbid state, 282
Preoccupation, 29, 131
Preparation, 20
Prescription, 186
Presence, 47, 68, 194, 234
Present, 38, 107, 142, 196, 213, 278
Pretense, 27, 51
Price, 178, 186
Priority, 233, 237
Privilege, 271

Prize, 186, 217
Problem, 5, 226
Procrastination, 172
Profit, 145, 192
Progeny, 197
Promise, 18, 21, 55, 246
Promissory, 55
Property, 104
Protect, 13
Psychosomatic, 94
PTSD, 156n
Pull, 60, 226
Puppeteer, 143
Push, 27, 100, 226

Quality, 87, 218
Quandary, 173
Question, 28, 72, 89, 122, 148, 177, 185, 234

Rabbit hole, 148
Race, 8, 194, 200
Raft, 11, 286
Rage, 58
Railway, 236
Rain, 61, 92
Rationality, 133
Raw, 235
Read, 9, 13, 32, 61, 148, 188, 255

Reality, 13, 14, 23, 27, 36, 50, 67, 68, 85, 87, 103, 107, 112, 130, 158, 179, 188, 196, 205, 208, 213, 221, 229, 233, 234, 241
Reason, 233, 257, 279
Recast perspective, 25, 120, 197, 215
Reception, 112
Recipe, 49
Reciprocate, 18, 40
Recognition, 140, 263
Recompense, 234
Record, 126, 215, 273
Recovery, 16, 92, 280
Recrimination, 215
Red herring, 94
Relationship, 6, 10, 14, 18, 25, 27, 30, 35, 36, 37, 40, 50, 58, 60, 71, 72, 74, 79, 88, 89, 91, 96, 102, 106, 108, 114, 118, 121, 124, 125, 126, 128, 135, 137, 141, 143, 146, 152, 155, 156, 158, 160, 162, 174, 178, 179, 182, 183, 184, 190, 194, 195, 202, 203, 210, 211, 214, 227, 231, 232, 233, 235, 237, 240, 241, 242, 243, 249, 252, 255, 256, 259, 264, 269, 272, 283, 286
Relatives, 125, 250
Relentless, 24
Religion, 8, 194, 254
Renewal, 243
Rent, 138
Repetition, 120
Reproduction, 253
Resentment, 57
Resident, 92, 98
Resilience, 2, 105
Resolution, 40, 229
Resources, 8, 115, 244
Respect, 58, 96, 118, 249
Responsibility, 206
Resumé padding, 97
Retro-fit, 179
Retrospective, 276
Revelation, 35
Rhythm, 266
Rich, 271
Riddle, 250
Right, 16, 100, 181, 200, 209, 224, 233, 279
Ritual, 48
River, 243
Rock, 226

Romance, 106, 234
Rope, 23, 286
Rose, 225
Roulette, 62
Routledge, Patricia, 33n

S, 45n
Sacrifice, 260
Sage, 153, 199, 214
Sail, 166
Sand, 114, 172, 184, 226, 265
Sanity, 14
Sanmitsu, 190
Savior, 50, 61, 145
Scab, 35
Schulberg, Budd, 236n
Screw others, 22
Seasons, 11
Secret, 117, 129
Sect, 8
Self, 7, 12, 13, 23, 29, 33, 35, 36, 60, 71, 95, 100, 108, 109, 112, 117, 126, 136, 141, 145, 152, 162, 164, 166, 178, 184, 207, 214, 218, 220, 234, 237, 238, 239, 240, 250, 271, 280, 283
Self-control, 257, 259
Self-counsel, 239
Self-entrapment, 29
Self-esteem, 164
Self-farmer, 60
Self-help, 100
Self-interest, 206, 260
Self-reflection, 136, 109n, 207, 280
Self-worth, 12, 117, 164, 166, 178, 237
Semiotics, 226
Sender, 238
Sense, 23, 34, 188
Senses, 30, 47, 241
Serendipity, 10, 148
Serfdom, 129
Servitude, 150
Sex, 22, 30, 40, 84, 106, 118, 130, 131, 137, 141, 143, 155, 194, 227, 231, 233, 242, 256, 259, 270, 284
Shackles, 283
Shade, 230
Shady, 9
Shakti, 110
Shatter-proof, 172
Sheep, 245
Shopping, 116
Shoulder, 111
Show, 33, 141, 143, 240

Shred, 14, 164, 268
Shun, 5
Sight, 5, 13, 179, 192, 216, 229
Signature, 32
Silence, 72
Simplicate, 132
Sin, 159
Single, 126, 139, 152
Sink, 97, 159, 284
Sister, 225
Situational awareness, 179, 187, 188, 241
Skills, 2, 174
Sky, 208, 277, 284
Slander, 124
Slap, 112
Slave, 261
Sleep, 37, 147, 148, 176
Slipper, 112
Smell, 251, 284
Snow, 11, 243n
Society, 13, 121, 139
Software, 266
Soldier, 67, 192
Soothsayer, 148
Sorcerer, 214
Sorrow, 68, 220n
Sou, 34
Soul, 10, 35, 45, 58, 68, 96, 106, 114, 118, 225n, 233, 236, 262, 282, 283
South, 84, 121n, 150, 151, 208, 270, 284, 285
Space, 29, 76, 79, 115, 129, 190, 229, 231
Spark, 6, 61
Species, 110
Spectrum, 1, 12, 200, 229, 230
Speech, 190
Sperm, 253
Spice, 89
Spindle, 274
Spirit, 68, 118, 258
Spoilt, 280
Spouse, 89
Spring, 243
SSM, 41n, 169n
Stalemate, 172
Stanley, Bessie, 278n
Star, 72, 143, 148, 240
Statistic, 266
Status quo, 218
Steward, 21
Stimulation, 117
Stocco, A, 204n
Stock, 155
Story, 33, 188, 273
Stout, William Bushnell, 132n
Stranger, 161, 280

Stranger at Home, 156n
Street cred, 112
Strength, 110, 218, 278, 280
Strlic, Matija, 251n
Struggle, 248
Student, 118
Styx, 248
Sublime, 284
Submission, 240
Subversive, 241
Subway, 231
Suicide, 68
Suit, 135
Suite, 135
Suitors, 135
Summer, 11, 76, 208, 270
Sun, 65, 76, 120, 176, 208, 262, 264
Sundress, 65
Superlatives, 36, 52
Supervision, 180
Support, 261
Suppression, 134, 136
Surrogate, 23
Survivor, 64, 180
Swim, 24, 220n
Sword, 5
Syncretic, 80

Talent, 277

TAP, 209n
Tattoo, 30
Tax sinks, 97
Tea, 48, 148, 262, 263
Teacher, 118, 212, 265
Teen, 112
Teles, 174
Temporary, 258
Temptation, 133, 257
Tense, 27, 34
Tension, 108
terra firma, 240
Thanks, 140
Thanksgiving, 102
Theology, 223
Theoretician, 240
They, 269
This, then that, 8
Thought, 1, 32, 36, 42, 59, 76, 80, 114, 131, 143, 163, 174, 190, 220, 238, 242
Thought-server, 238
Three Marriages, 108
Tide, 226
Time, 29, 60, 108, 115, 176, 182, 195, 229, 264, 276
Timing, 195
Tincture of time, 66
Today, 24, 49
Toxic, 50n, 106
Trace, 277

Tracker, 11
Trail, 277
Train, 94, 192, 231, 236, 271
Trap, 2, 29, 59, 72, 136
Trapdoor, 59
Traveler, 17, 101, 231
Treatment, 94
Trees, 38
Trifecta, 27
Trigger, 25
Troll, 82
Tru dat, 200
Trust, 218, 243, 252, 254
Truth, 50, 85, 145, 183, 193, 233, 236, 245, 271
Tumbleweed, 264
Tummy, 78
Tush, 100
Tutor, 135
Two-faced, 50
Tyranny, 280

Umbilical cord, 253
Undeliverable, 60, 159
Unequal, 111
Unexpected, 20
Unfiltered, 235
Unforgiven, 228
Unformalized, 121

Unhappiness, 101, 243, 262
Unified, 84
Union, 106
Universe, 206, 240, 277
Unlock, 283
Unreality, 205, 233
Unwieldy, 99
Unworthy, 271
USM, 153n
Utopia, 67, 68
Valentine, 255
Validation, 165
Vapors, 258
Venal, 5, 218, 246
Venn diagram, 109n
Version, 107, 196, 238
Vicious, 5, 218, 246
Vihar, 44
Viral, 130
Virgo, 148
Virtual, 196
Virtual reality, 234
Virtue, 147
Virus, 227
Visionary, 92n
Vitriol, 82
Vocabulary, 36
Voice, 30, 68, 102, 180, 273

Wallet, 173

Wanderlust, 101
War, 8, 192
Warmth, 233
Warning, 212
Waterwheel, 211
Way, 55, 218, 247
Weak, 5, 218, 246, 278
Weapon, 5, 8, 192
Weary, 168
Weave, 273, 274
Web, 29
Wedge, 99
Weed, 117
Weeds, 60
Weight, 59, 257
West, 84
Westerlies, 208
Wetware, 266
White, 208
Whore, 131
Whyte, David, 108n
Wife, 50, 155
Wi-Fi, 112
Wilde, Oscar, 4n
Williams, Robin, 270n
Willie, 169
Willpower, 257
Winner, 62
Winter, 11

Wireless, 112
Wisdom, 4, 32, 80, 214, 278
Wish, 213
Wolf, 245
Woman, 39, 112, 269
Womb, 38
Woods, 38
Work, 57, 64, 108, 162, 168, 261, 274, 277
Work-Life balance, 109n
World, 54, 56, 109
World view, 56
Worry, 172
Worth, 160, 178, 237
Wrap, 174
Wreck, 14, 243
Wrong, 56, 233

Yard, 31, 260
Yellow, 65
Yiddish, 57
Youth, 231
Yo-yo, 36

Zebra, 94

Title Index

8-22-8, 274
99 And Counting, 280
A 15 Minute Hug, 96
A Mentor, 86
A Plea To Paenibacillus, 170
A Question Or, My Life, According To Electrons, 234
A Suite For Suitors, 135
A Time For Everything, 195
Ability, 115
Accounting Error, 19
Address Not Found . . ., 238
Age And Experience, 168
Am I Your Friend?, 87
Anchored Friends, 107
Anticipatory Anxiety, 94
Antidote For Paranoia, 20
Anxiety, 255
Appearances To Keep, 33
Archivist Or Arsonist—A Choice, 71
Ardent Lover, 51
Arrival Equals Departure, 47
Ask Not Guess, 128
Aspire, 275
At the Hospital Of No Return, 248
Au Naturel, 31
Authenticity Of Rawness, 235
Authority Figures, 138
Awake In The Wake Of A Shooting Star, 240
Backed Up, 136
BC And AD Meet BC And AC, 213
Behold! I Flow!, 39
Best Fit, 244
Bin There—Dun That, 109

Bipolar Vocabulary, 36
Call It As It Is, 52
Cancer, 157
Caution! Eavesdropper On-Board, 197
Caveat Emptor!, 212
China Syndrome AKA Law Of Unintended Consequences, 129
Clarity Of Distance, 114
Cohabitants!, 137
Consider A Void . . ., 229
Control The Troll—I & II, 82
Controlled Flight Into Terrain (CFIT), 179
Convenience Trap, 2
Cord Of Life, 253
Cross-sectionist—Longitudinalist—*And/Or*?, 188
Crowd Control, 150
Day Dreams, 176
Dead-End, 272
Dear Lover Dear, 214
Death Of A Teacher, 265
Debtor For Life, 171
Delayed Union, 106
Depression, 134
Design My Funeral?, 223
Did It Happen?, 91
Did You Feel It?, 249
Discussion—The Lack Thereof, 5
Does It Matter?, 283
Double-Speak, 50
Early Morning Memories, 76
Either—And—Neither, 199
Empathy For Realists, 85
Enough Is Not Enough Or Is It?, 18

Eyes Tell No Lies, 126
Face Value, 9
Faces Of A Lie, 183
False Expectations, 169
Family And Friends, 203
Fantasy Or Reality, 103
Fantasy, 21
Fat Head, 75
First Day, 161
Found And Not Easily Lost, 166
Frenzied Love, 237
Gender Discrimination Need Not Apply, 93
Giving Is Not A Given, 12
Gone Away, 196
Habit Forming Humans, 144
Hair Of The Goat, 285
Hair-trigger, 177
Halo Family, 202
Healing Can't Come Fast Enough, 66
Hot And Frozen, 6
Hot Cup Of Tea, 262
How Nice, 140
Humanity's Essence, 162
I Watched, 58
IBGYBG, 206
Identity Crisis, Unidentified, 28
In An Infinite Loop, 198
In Good Faith, 111
Incoming, 54
Inconvenient Lie, 236
Indigent Get It, Don't Patronize, 145
Indulge Not Bulge, 78
Infinite Prejudice, 200

Infinite Shade, 230
Inheritance, 104
Interns' Lament, 98
Inviting The Uninvited, 74
Journey's End, 252
Keep It Close, 22
Keep It Real, 205
Keep It Simple, 124
Know This, 120
Know Thy Enemy—The Elephant In The Room, 192
Know Thyself, 117
Know Thyself!, 207
Knowledge, 99
Ladder Of Life, 217
Laying Of The Feet—Yours, 23
Laying Of The Hands—Yours, 23
Least Bad One, 204
Leave No Trace, 277
Leave Your Mark, 222
Let Sleeping Dogs Lie, 147
Let Sleeping Dogs Lie, Again, 148
Letting Go, Not Goodbye, 286
Life Cycles, 38
Like A Lump, 210
Liquor As Metaphor, 90
Lost And Not Easily Found, 164
Louisiana—Revisited, 151
Love In Three Acts, 88
Love Me . . .,131
Loveless, 211
Lovers, 231
Lower Latitude Lover, 284
Makes Sense, 34

Marriageable Age, 139
Matrimonial Bliss, 269
Matter Of Course, 125
Means To An End—An Aviation Metaphor, 279
Memories Are Forever . . ., 32
Memory—Trick Or Treat?, 46
Metaphoric Hot Cup Of Tea, 263
Missing A Match, 256
More Perspective On Perspective, 187
Morning Ritual, 48
Moving Blues, 154
Moving On, 232
Multiple Personalities And Counting, 158
Mummy's Recipe Book, 49
My Drink and I, 220
My Gifts . . ., 276
My Kind Of Optimist, 224
My Warmth Returns, 233
My World View Or Delusions Of Grandeur, 56
NASDeC, 155
Never Again, 246
No Buyer's Remorse, 83
No Strings Attached, 143
Noblesse Oblige, 97
Non, 70
Not In Any Dictionary, 121
Not This Time, 62
Now, Not Later, 282
Nursing Hope, 16
Oh, Humankind, 8
Oh! So Pavlovian, 26
Older ≠ Wiser, 80
On My Way Out, 42

Parting Shot, 242
Partner In Absentia, 122
Perception Of Forgiveness, 228
Perspective, 186
Pigeonhole, 191
Power Of Prayer, 254
Prayer For Freedom, 281
Promissory Or Pro-misery, 55
Pull And Push, 226
Quandary Of Laundry, 173
Rain, The Great Motivator, 92
Recasting Perspective, 25
Relationship Want Ad, 194
Relationships, Require Relating, 40
Revelation, 35
S's poem, 44
Sacrificing Your Ease For The Common Good Or Not In My Backyard, 260
Savior, Heed This, 61
Selective Resiliency, 105
Self-entrapment Or Isolation, 29
Self-Farmer, 60
Self-help With No Help, 100
Shakti—*Almost*, 110
Show Me, In The Light, 141
Shredding Paper, Only, 268
Simplicate, And Then Add Lightness, 132
Single, 152
Six Days Later—Was That You?, 208
Speak Oracle!, 241
Spoilt, 280
STOP!, 64
Suitor Of Any Gender, 135

Suitor Of Other Genders, 135
Suitor, 135
Summery Sunday Siesta, 270
Survivor, 180
Take Heed, No Second Edition, 239
Teen Daymare, 112
Temptation Of Rationality, 133
Thanksgiving, 102
The Ark Of Life, 4
The Block In Thought, 1
The Case Against Insensate Intelligence, 266
The Dice In Our Lives, 10
The Dilemma, 7
The Earth, And 10 Things I Got For Free, 250
The Eulogy, 225
The Fever, 227
The Guilt Of Conscience, 59
The Human Condition, 15
The Hurricane, 14
The Impasse, 172
The Importance Of *And*, 185
The Ledger, 215
The Olfactory Connection, 251
The Optimistic Pessimist, 221
The Organized Person, 116
The Papers, 184
The Path(s) Taken, 163
The Price Of Living, 178
The Protected—A Public Service Reminder, For Parents, Politicians, And Policymakers, 13
The Public Phone Booth, 79
The Resentment, 57
The Tension, 108

The Truth About Altruism, 193
The Truth Comes Bedraggled, 271
The Undoing, 156
The Unified States Of Orgasm, 84
The Unwrapping, 174
Then And Now, 37
This And That Way, 218
This Is Love Too, 11
Three C's, 190
Time Flies, 264
Traveler, 17
Trifecta, 27
Two Questions For Spouses, 89
Tyranny of Longevity, 280
Undeliverable, 159
Universality Of Energy, 153
Unmoved, 146
Unrelenting And Determining, 24
Utopian Dream—Dystopian Reality, 67
Utopian Dream—Dystopian Reality, Revisited, 68
Vapors, 258
Virality Of Fantasy, 130
Voice To Love, 30
Wait Not, Want Now, 182
Waiting For The Spring Flood, 243
Wanderlust, 101
Way It Is, Always, 142
We Are Links In The Chain Of Continuity, 278
We Can Have It All, 261
Weaver Of The Historical Record, 273
Weight Of Comfort, 257
What I Really Need Is—, 118
Where Did I Misplace It?, 216

Wolf In Sheep's Clothing, 245
Worth Or The Absence Thereof, 160
Yellow, The Warm Color Of Love, 65
Yet Again, 72
Young Love, 259

Printed in the USA
CPSIA information can be obtained
at www.ICGtesting.com
CBHW041913291024
16595CB00014B/187